INNOVATIVE STRETCHCORD TRAINING

for

SWIMMERS

by

Alan W. Arata, Ph.D.

© 2006 by Alan W. Arata. All rights reserved.

No part of this book may be reproduced, stored in a retrieval system, or transmitted by any means, electronic, mechanical, photocopying, recording, or otherwise, without written permission from the author.

First published by AuthorHouse 2/21/06

ISBN: 1-4259-2085-3(e-book)
ISBN: 1-4259-2084-5(paperback)

This book is printed on acid free paper.

Printed in the United States of America

Cover photograph and artwork by © Alan Arata, 2006

The word StrechCordz® refers specifically to the resistance band devices made by NZ MFG LLC, Tallmadge OH and will appear in this book with the trademark. The word stretchcords is a domain name with an implied trademark from NZ MFG LLC, Tallmadge OH. With permission from NZ MFG, it (and stretchcord) will be used generically to refer to resistance band devices and will appear in the title and text without the trademark symbol.

Acknowledgements

I would like to give my sincerest thanks to my wife, Kim Arata who spent hundreds of hours editing, Rob Clayton, Head Men's Swim Coach for the United States Air Force Academy, and Pat Hogan, USA Swimming Club Development Director for their many hours of review, insight and editing. Because of the input of these individuals, new ideas have been brought forward to help this book show even more innovations. I am respectfully grateful.

I would also like to thank the individuals who served as models for the illustrations: Kristen, Kim, Bryce, Ryan, Meghan & Kevin.

TABLE OF CONTENTS

TABLE OF CONTENTS   4

INTRODUCTION   1

THE STRETCHCORD   4

THE INVENTION OF STRETCHCORDS   5
WHY USE STRETCHCORDS   6
TYPES OF STRETCHCORDS   9

DRYLAND TRAINING   12

MUSCLE ADAPTATION   12
MUSCULAR STRENGTH, POWER AND ENDURANCE   17
OVERLOAD PRINCIPLE   18
TRAINING FOR POWER   20
PERIODIZATION   22

CHILDREN AND STRETCHCORDS   25

HOW MUCH, HOW OFTEN   28

USING STRETCHCORDS   33

STROKES ON STRETCHCORDS   36

STRETCHCORD SWIMMING   37

BUTTERFLY	37
BACKSTROKE	40
BREASTSTROKE	42
FREESTYLE	45
VARYING THE RESISTANCE	49

OTHER STRETCHCORD EXERCISES   51

FOREARM MUSCLES WORKOUT	51
THE CATCH	53
LEG WORKOUTS	53
SQUATS	54
GROIN WORK	55
KICKING	57
INJURY PREVENTION/REHABILITATION	59

DESIGNING WORKOUTS   62

OFF-SEASON TRAINING	67
BASE/TECHNIQUE TRAINING	69
RACE SPECIFIC TRAINING	72
TAPER	74
FUN TRAINING	76

TRIATHLON TRAINING   79

THE FREESTYLE PULL PATTERN	82

WORLD CLASS STRETCHCORD ROUTINES   85

WOMEN'S 50M FREESTYLE	87
MEN'S 50M FREESTYLE	87
WOMEN'S 100M FREESTYLE	88
MEN'S 100M FREESTYLE	88
WOMEN'S 200M FREESTYLE	89
MEN'S 200M FREESTYLE	89
WOMEN'S DISTANCE FREE	90
MEN'S DISTANCE FREE	90
WOMEN'S 100M BACKSTROKE	91

MEN'S 100M BACKSTROKE	91
WOMEN'S 200M BACKSTROKE	92
MEN'S 200M BACKSTROKE	92
WOMEN'S 100M BREASTSTROKE	93
MEN'S 100M BREASTSTROKE	93
WOMEN'S 200M BREASTSTROKE	94
MEN'S 200M BREASTSTROKE	94
WOMEN'S 100M BUTTERFLY	95
MEN'S 100M BUTTERFLY	95
WOMEN'S 200M BUTTERFLY	96
MEN'S 200M BUTTERFLY	96
WOMEN'S 200M IM	97
MEN'S 200M IM	97
WOMEN'S 400 IM	98
MEN'S 400 IM	99

STRETCHCORD WRAP-UP   100

REFERENCES   102

GLOSSARY OF TERMS   103

ABOUT THE AUTHOR   106

INTRODUCTION

A swimmer concentrates on her form. Both arms and both hands, outstretched above her head, move first into a water grabbing position. With elbows high, her hands travel together down the centerline of her body. As they do, she can feel the muscles in her forearms, her triceps and the muscles of her back burn as she pushes through past her waist then extends her elbows so that her hands pass just beyond her hips. She glances up and takes a breath as her arms recover to the extended position where she started. She thinks to herself, "five strokes to go".

If when reading this, you got the impression this swimmer was swimming butterfly—you're close. In fact, she was working out with stretchcords, mimicking the butterfly stroke, exercising the same muscles in the same sequence required to swim butterfly. She was doing "dryland training" with stretchcords.

My experience as a swimmer, a swim coach, a biology professor and a doctor of biomechanics have solidified my belief that proper dryland training can greatly enhance swimming performance. Because so little good information exists for swimmers and coaches who want to start a dryland training program, I began putting together a dryland training book specifically *for* swimmers. I was quickly struck by the knowledge that no one would be able to do *all* the dryland training in the book's pages. I knew that I would have to recommend *specific* dryland training programs for the book to have any practical value. With this in mind, I put stretchcord training at the top of the list of dryland exercises I would recommend to the vast majority of swimmers, and decided to dedicate an entire book to the use of these resistance band devices, including some innovations that I have come up with over the years.

I do believe stretchcord training can be the single best dryland training for most swimmers. I also like plyometrics and core body training, but I believe stretchcord training should be the *cornerstone* dryland program for swimmers. My appreciation for stretchcords is based on a number of criteria. First and foremost, stretchcords work the muscles with increasing resistance in a near identical way to actual swimming. Muscles can work the same way with stretchcords as they work in the water, both in activation patterns and actual power needed to complete an arm pull. Because of this, stretchcord training *out* of the water can be used to improve actual swimming technique *in* the water. Stretchcords are also light, transportable, inexpensive, and come in varying resistances. In summary, they're ideal for exercising the right muscles with the right amount of resistance, they can be used almost anywhere, and they are cost effective. Stretchcords are just about perfect.

Among other things, this book is designed to teach swimmers the proper way to perform stretchcord training. Proper technique while performing stretchcord training should translate to proper form in the water while swimming. This book should also give coaches and swimmers ideas on how to incorporate a stretchcord program into their yearly training cycle. Additionally, this book will illustrate innovative ways to use stretchcords to better train all strokes, as well as suggest workouts to help swimmers mimic specific swimming races, including stroke counts and tempos. No other dryland training program really does this. So, whether you are an age group, master or triathlete swimmer, read on and get ready for a dryland program that is challenging, fun, and should significantly improve your swimming performance.

ONE

THE STRETCHCORD

Land-based training is often referred to as "dryland training" and can be defined as any training that takes place out of the water designed to increase swimming velocity in the water. Although dryland training can vary from running to core body strength programs, many swimmers think of *resistance* training (like weight or stretchcord training) when they hear the words *dry* and *land* used together.

Swimmers, coaches and researchers often disagree about what type of dryland training is best for swimmers. But nearly everyone involved in exercise agrees that the concept of *training specificity*, which states that the best way to train for a specific activity is to do *that* activity, is an overriding principle in any good training program. What this means is that swimming and swimming-like movements are the activities that will best improve swimming. Nothing beats practicing swimming for improving swimming speed. In general, dryland training should not be used to *replace* swimming unless necessitated by an injury. Instead, dryland training should be used to *complement* swim practice training.

One of the best dryland swim training devices ever invented is the elastic band device swimmers usually refer to as the stretchcord.

Loosely defined, a stretchcord is a band that provides resistance when stretched. Stretchcord resistance stresses pulling muscles and, with proper rest, these muscles adapt to that stress, becoming stronger in that particular range of motion. If that motion is similar to a swimming motion, then the muscles are stronger for swimming and have the potential to produce more force in the water, which should translate to faster swimming.

Producing more force in the water is one of the two ways a swimmer can swim faster (Arata, 2003). To increase swimming speed, swimmers can either, 1) produce more propulsive force, or 2) reduce drag. These are the only two ways a swimmer can actually move faster through the water. Stretchcord training can help increase flexibility and thereby reduce drag, but primarily stretchcord training increases strength in the specific muscles used during swimming. Moreover, since stretchcord training is accomplished using a swimming-like motion, the sequence of muscle activation is nearly identical to that of actual swimming. Both of these factors (specific muscle strength and specific motion training) can give swimmers who train with stretchcords the ability to apply more propulsive force on the water when they swim. This is why stretchcords work so effectively.

The Invention of Stretchcords

Stretchcord training is not new. In fact, swimmers have been using stretchcords for many decades. Some of the first stretchcords were made of medical-type surgical tubing. Swimmers would tie loops in both ends, put the tubing around a pole (the pool exit ladder perhaps), place their hands in the loops, back up and start pulling. This kind of tubing can still be used today and would still be effective. Medical supply stores carry surgical tubing by the roll. All one needs to know is how long they want the cords to be.

As with any good idea, stretchcords have become a bit more advanced. Today, stretchcords made specifically for swimming can be purchased ready-to-use. Some of these cords include plastic handles or paddles, much like swim paddles. Some have straps at the halfway point to help tie them off, which prevents them from breaking as easily as the medical tubing, given this is a critical stress point in the system. Commercially designed stretchcords also come in varying band thicknesses, and they are designed to withstand continued pulling unlike surgical tubing, which is generally designed to restrict blood flow (if you've had your blood drawn then you've had surgical tubing placed around your arm). Because of the varying thicknesses available, swimmers don't need to *over*-stretch *commercially* purchased stretchcords, making them not only more functional, but less likely to snap. It is worth the relatively small price to buy good stretchcords.

Why Use Stretchcords

Some of the following has been said before, but it is worth repeating. The best things about stretchcords are that they provide great resistance training while allowing swimmers to come very close to mimicking proper swimming arm motions in all four strokes. Generally, the more any dryland work approximates swimming motions, the more likely it will produce faster swimming. Not only can stretchcord work mirror proper swimming technique, proper technique used during stretchcord training can translate to a proper swimming stroke in the water. This is the case because stretchcord work strengthens movement patterns. Swimmers tend to use pull patterns in the water that *feel* strong to them. So, it is important that swimmers mimic proper pull patterns in the four competitive strokes when using stretchcords. Pulling *incorrectly* with stretchcords, just as pulling incorrectly in the water could cause more harm than good, because incorrect repetitions will build strength in incorrect motor patterns, and those incorrect forms will become habit the water. Therefore, it cannot be stressed enough that all stretchcord pulls should be done using proper stroke technique. The old adage that, "Practice doesn't make perfect—it makes *permanent*," is oh so true.

Of course, by their very nature, stretchcords provide more resistance the further they are stretched. This means that throughout a stretchcord pull, the tension increases. The end of a pull is more difficult than the beginning. This is different than a weight machine that provides consistent resistance throughout a motion. I highlight this aspect of stretchcords because it is a great benefit. When a swimmer strokes in the water, the beginning of their pull is stronger than the end of their pull because mechanically, swimmers are able to activate more muscle fibers to perform the swimming task in the catch phase of the stroke as compared to the "finish" of the stroke. When swimmers tire or slow down, it is often commented that, "their strokes shortened." What actually became shorter were the *ends* of their strokes. They physically didn't have enough strength to *finish* their pulls. Using stretchcords will help strengthen the *finishes* of swimmers' strokes because of the greater resistance at the end of a stretchcord pull. Swimmers who work with stretchcords should benefit from this specific-area strength gain.

Along a similar line, one racing technique used in swimming is to finish through the ends of the strokes very *fast* so that the hands can get back to the catch position quickly. It takes a great deal of strength to *accelerate* the hand through the end of a swimming stroke. The ever-increasing resistance aspect of stretchcords again, can develop the strength needed to do this, perhaps even better than swimming itself can.

Stretchcord workouts are not limited by the size of the pool. In a pool, swimmers can only take so many strokes before they are forced to turn. During the turn, their arms are necessarily at rest, which can hamper training. This is especially true for swimmers training in a short course pool, but needing to compete in either long course or open water. With stretchcord training, swimmers can pull continuously for the number of pulls that best suits the event or events for which they are training.

One last asset of stretchcords is their portability. They are small and light and can be used just about anywhere. If a swimmer is going on vacation, or in the case of a masters swimmer, perhaps a business trip, a set of stretchcords takes up little more room than a pair of shoes. They can be tied off to door handles, banister rails, and in some cases heavy furniture. They can be used in hotels, at grandma's house, even in airports. No reason to leave them at home. This means a training routine doesn't have to stop because the equipment or pool is not available.

Cost is also a consideration when looking at any kind of training. There are other dryland swim devices, like the Swim Bench® that do a good job mimicking the swimming stroke, at least for freestyle and butterfly. Swim Benches® also have some nice technological features (isokinetic resistance and force gauges) that increase their usefulness. However, these swimming-specific training devices can cost thousands of dollars. And despite their much lower cost, stretchcords have advantages in several areas.

So, stretchcords are ideal for dryland swim training because they offer resistance training that mimics the swimming stroke, and the resistance increases throughout each pull. The facts that they are inexpensive, they travel light and can be used nearly anywhere are added benefits in a sport that thrives on daily training.

Types of Stretchcords

There are several companies that manufacture resistance band training devices. Because of this, I am often asked, "What type of resistance bands should a swimmer buy?" Here I will speak from personal experience. I have used a number of different products over the years, but I purchase StrechCordz® for my swimmers and myself. There are several reasons that many coaches strongly prefer the StrechCordz® brand and why it's the only brand most swim shops carry. First, the superior quality means better workouts and less likelihood of cord failure. NZ Manufacturing (the maker of StrechCordz®) has developed several innovations in safety that are not available in other resistance band devices. Most resistance bands are developed for recreational, occasional use. They wear out, not from use, but from disuse. They become brittle and lose their elasticity over time. Swimmers use stretchcords for very serious training, placing a much higher demand on the tubing. Therefore, stretchcords developed for the needs of swimmers must be made to higher standards. It would not be uncommon for a single set of cords to be pulled 2000 times in one day by a collegiate or club team. The local general fitness store does not carry resistance bands designed to repeatedly take this type of load.

StrechCordz® come with a choice of handles or paddles. Some swimmers are more comfortable using the paddles. Swimmers who are working on their technique or who have trouble keeping their hands in a flat, relaxed position while swimming should strongly consider getting the ones with paddles. Those who are only using the cords for strength gain can go with either option.

In addition, StrechCordz® come in the correct length for swimming arm pull motions. Some other resistance bands are short, so their resistance increases too much during a pull. Other bands are too long and don't provide enough resistance increase. Also, these bands do not have the research and development behind them directed towards improved swimming performance. For these reasons, I recommend StrechCordz® from NZ MFG. They can be purchased at nearly every swim shop or directly from NZ at www.nzmfg.com.

Another question often asked is, "What level of resistance should I get?" The following is a set of recommendations based on experiences with age group through college swimmers. Masters swimmers and triathletes should put themselves in the appropriate group according to their level of strength.

StrechCordz® come in five different colors, depending on their resistance. The colors are silver, yellow, green, red and blue from least to most resistance. The following chart should help swimmers select the right strength StrechCordz®.

Silver	Extra Light	10 & under swimmers, rehabilitation for all swimmers
Yellow	Light	13 & under swimmers
Green	Medium	Post-puberty males and strong females Short, high intensity bouts for 11 – 13 year olds
Red	Heavy	Strong adult or college females, high school males Short, high intensity bouts for green cord users
Blue	Extra Heavy	Adult or college males, very strong high school males Short, high intensity bouts for red cord users

TWO

DRYLAND TRAINING

As mentioned earlier, the goal of a dryland training program is to increase velocity in the water. This usually means physically changing swimmers' bodies to create greater forces. While I want to avoid making this book a physiology tome, I feel it is essential to include a short section on how muscles adapt to resistance training. One goal of this book is to empower the reader to better understand his/her own body and what type of exercises and routines might work best towards strength gain. Future pages do list a variety of workouts, but there is no way any book is intended to custom design an individual program for each and every reader. If a reader, however, understands some general principles of strength development, then that reader can develop training routines tailored to any specific need. "Give a man a fish and feed him for a day, or *teach* a man to fish and feed him for a lifetime," is the philosophy of this book. So, read on.

Muscle Adaptation

The human body is amazing in its ability to adapt to the stresses and loads placed upon it. This ability to adapt is what makes *training* for swimming or any other sport meaningful. Adaptations to training include bigger and or stronger muscles, tendons, ligaments and bones. Adaptations also occur in the nervous, circulatory and other body systems, some that are not normally associated with improved performance by the average swimmer, but that are essential to improved swimming performance nonetheless.

Many people exercise to develop bigger muscles. While larger muscles may come with training, it is not the size of the muscle upon which a swimmer should concentrate, but the strength or power the muscle can generate. Still, as increased muscle size generally comes with training, it is good to have an understanding of how muscle size increases.

Muscles are comprised of (among other things) two different types of protein fibers called actin and myosin. When these fibers are stressed (by a workout for instance), they tend to react to that stress by getting bigger over time. This is known as *hypertrophy*. There is also evidence that when these fibers are placed under stress they can split and lay down more actin and myosin, thereby essentially making *more* muscle—more fibers (Gonyea at el, 1986). This is called *hyperplasia* and is becoming more accepted by the scientific community. For this book, whether a muscle increases in size through hypertrophy or hyperplasia is not important. In fact, whether a muscle gets bigger at all is not really important. What *is* important is that a muscle becomes more powerful. And increases in muscle power can occur with or without increases in size. This is something that is important to understand, because many swimmers, especially female swimmers, *don't* get bigger muscles with increased training nor do they really want to. Swimmers want the greatest strength to body ratio possible. Stretchcords facilitate this by working the most primary muscles associated with swimming. They do not "bulk up" the muscles that don't contribute to swimming propulsion, such as the bench press exercise would.

In addition to a change in muscle strength, other training related changes occur within the body. The bloodstream carries oxygen and nutrients to the muscles. When muscles *work*, the increased need for oxygen triggers the human body to produce, 1) more red blood cells and 2) more blood. These adaptations help swimmers' endurance and can occur with stretchcord training and swim training alike.

Both swimming and stretchcord workouts make the heart work harder. The heart muscle, like any other muscle in the body, adapts to stress by growing larger and stronger. A stronger heart with larger blood chambers means more blood is pumped with each heartbeat, taking more nutrients and more oxygen to muscles and body tissues. When the heart works in an "aerobic" way (using oxygen to produce energy), such as in swimming, the heart muscle not only gets larger and stronger, the amount of blood it can pump in one beat increases because the chambers of the heart (the atria and ventricles) increase in size (Wilmore & Costill, 1994). This is very beneficial. When an athlete only lifts weights and does so in short quick bursts *without* any aerobic work, the heart muscle itself will respond by getting bigger. However, the amount of blood the heart can pump does not increase because the heart chamber sizes do not increase. This "anaerobic" work (without oxygen) does not significantly increase the need for oxygen to the body tissues, thus no adaptation of the chamber sizes occur. This greater heart size, but not blood-moving-capacity adaptation is not usually a healthy one. Stretchcords can potentially produce *both* types of adaptations depending on their usage.

There are two general types of muscle fibers within skeletal (or movement) muscles, *slow twitch* and *fast twitch*. Slow twitch muscle fibers are associated with endurance (aerobic) efforts, while fast twitch muscle fibers are associated with (anaerobic) sprints. Each of these muscle fiber types can be specifically trained, to improve endurance or sprint capacity respectively.

Swim meets may be all *sprint, sprint, sprint,* but swim *workouts* are filled with predominantly less intense efforts. Most swim workouts are designed to stress muscles aerobically, which works on endurance/slow twitch fibers. One of the most significant ways muscles adapt to aerobic work is by increasing the number of mitochondria (the powerhouses of cells), which allows them to produce more energy with the help of the oxygen the swimmers breathe. This same type of training can be done with stretchcords. To accomplish it, swimmers perform multiple repetitions (~100) using lighter resistance stretchcords. After a short rest, swimmers may repeat the set several times.

A swimmer who has a leg injury could use a set like this to stay in upper body and aerobic shape while restricted from the water. Aerobic stretchcord training sets can also get a swimmer into shape before the season starts. As mentioned earlier, one of the great things about stretchcords is that they are small and can be used anywhere. So, even when a swimmer is on vacation or otherwise away from a pool, stretchcord training can be used as a substitute for swimming.

The second type of muscle fibers swimmers need to train is fast twitch. Fast twitch muscle fibers are anaerobic fibers, not requiring oxygen to contract. Without air, muscles get around 18 times less energy (fast twitch fibers are only 6% as efficient as slow twitch fibers when it comes to energy utilization). Also, fast twitch muscle fibers produce a substance known as lactic acid, the build-up of which is believed not only to cause muscle failure or fatigue but also physical discomfort—pain. Fast twitch fibers *are*, however, big, and can *produce* a lot of *force*, much more than slow twitch fibers. At a highly competitive level, swimming events 200 meters and below (that's most swimming events!) use significantly more *fast* than slow twitch fibers. Since swim practices are often designed to predominantly task *slow* twitch fibers, supplemental stretchcord training can greatly aid swimmers in force production potential for swimming races. More about how to train these fibers is written in the upcoming section, "Training for Power."

When swimmers train in or out of the water, concentration is often on muscular development. It's easy to understand why. It is in the muscles where a swimmer feels fatigue. But perhaps more important than muscular changes from training are neurological changes that occur. Exercise physiologists will usually say that improvements in a strength program gained during the first three weeks are the results of neurological adaptations rather than changes in the muscle fibers themselves. The brain sends signals to the muscles to contract, and those contractions create body movement—swimming in our case. There are multiple variations of neurological signals that occur between brain and muscle. And within a muscle, there are many different nerves that activate different sections of that muscle, creating different power outputs. When an individual first learns to swim, their stroke pattern is visibly erratic and the contractions of their muscles are not efficient. As they train (mostly with aerobic training), their neurological pathways become more defined. This improves the consistency, smoothness and efficiency of the swimmer's technique, often called their "feel of the water." A very important neurological adaptation to training is that more of the muscle fibers within a muscle contract when called upon. This helps the swimmer create more force or pull on the water. At the same time, scientists think that neurological training *limits* activation from muscles that are *not* needed for the movement. When we think of a talented swimmer, we think of someone with perfect strokes and no extraneous motions (they create the same stroke pattern with every pull). This is what swim training can do for a swimmer. And since stretchcord movement patterns are so similar to swimming patterns, it is also what *stretchcord training* can do for a swimmer.

Muscular Strength, Power and Endurance

In general, there are three ways to measure the strength of a muscle. What's called "muscular strength" can be determined with a one-time lift. This 1 RM, or *one rep max,* is the maximum weight that can be lifted in one attempt. "Muscular power" is determined by lifting a weight as *quickly* as possible. And "muscular endurance" is the ability to repeat an exercise over and over again.

Since swimming is a timed event, muscular power is more relevant than simple muscular strength. To train to increase muscular power one uses high resistance and few repetitions. Even the 50 freestyle, however, requires several pulls or repetitions per length with the same set of muscles. This means muscular endurance is also required. The number of push-ups a person can do is generally considered an excellent measure of that person's muscular endurance with respect to body weight. How many times does a 100 freestyler pull with the right arm during an all-out swim? All swimming races are muscular endurance events—longer events requiring more endurance than shorter ones. Stretchcord training is great for these types of events as long as swimmers can complete between 30 and 50 repetitions with the cords. This is why it is so important to choose cords with proper resistance. (Swimmers should choose cords with which they can perform 25-50 pulls with good form).

Muscular power and muscular endurance can be trained together. Using the push-up example, how *fast* can a person do, say *50* push-ups? This combination is important for swimming because races are timed—it is not, "can they do the strokes?" but "how fast can they do the strokes?" By being able to pull the hand through the water faster, swimmers generally *swim* faster. Pulling stretchcords at a given stroke rate (i.e. one pull every second), can help a swimmer gain muscular power as well as muscular endurance.

So, swimmers need muscular endurance to complete an event. In addition, they need muscular power to complete an event faster. This book details stretchcord workouts to help swimmers achieve either or both of these necessities for different swimming races.

Overload Principle

The goal when starting a swimming stretchcord program is to become better and faster at swimming. In order for this to take place, some change in the body must occur. When the human body is placed under stress, it either adapts or breaks down. This is the *Overload Principle*. Body systems must be used *more than normal* to improve. If muscles are not overloaded, no change will occur. This principle is what makes working out fruitful.

Muscles will usually get bigger/stronger until they reach the optimum size/strength for a specific task. In other words, if a swimmer did 200 stretchcord pulls every day for 4 straight months, then the muscles would adapt in both size and strength for that task. If the swimmer then started a stretchcord program of *400* pulls every day, the muscles would become stronger, adapting once again. Many in the past have wrongfully assumed that, "if some is good, more must be better—If 200 pulls make me strong and 400 pulls make me stronger, then 800 pulls will make me stronger yet." This is only true up to a point, and that point varies by individual. An ever-increasing overload of work cannot continue indefinitely, as eventually too many pulls will lead to injury.

Applying the Overload Principle to stretchcord training means that the muscles need to be stressed beyond that to which they are accustomed. This is not too difficult. If 100 stretchcord pulls are added to the daily routine, extra stress has been placed on the body. If this continues, then pretty soon, *it* is routine, and more or different types of exercises will need to be performed to see *continued* improvement.

Sooner or later in their careers, swimmers will plateau, meaning they will come to a point where their times stop improving. Swimmers in such a plateau stage can try changing their training routines, for instance stressing power over endurance or visa versa. Care should be taken not to overload the body beyond its capacity to heal, however. There is a fine line, a balancing act between being in the best shape and injury, which each individual must learn. The body needs time to recover. In general, endurance workouts, even though they may be longer, do not require as much recovery time as sprint/power workouts. The predominance of aerobic (endurance) effort in most swim workouts is why swimmers can swim every day—the 12-20 hours between workouts are enough for the body to recover. If swimmers do very high intensity work with stretchcords, however, very strenuous pulls until fatigue several times in a row, they will need more recovery time. Swimmers in general are used to working hard with little recovery. Because of this, they should take especial care to avoid overuse injuries when stretchcord training is introduced.

Training for Power

As already mentioned, there are two general types of muscle fibers in the body, fast twitch and slow twitch. Most discussions of muscle fiber include a third type titled, *Fast Oxidative Glycolitic,* or FOG fibers. Consider this third fiber a "tweener" fiber that has characteristics of both fast and slow twitch fibers. Slow twitch fibers are relatively small and excellent for endurance. Fast twitch fibers are larger and are good for developing power, though they fatigue quickly. FOG fibers can develop a great deal of power as well, but are also somewhat resistant to fatigue. This is the fiber most swimmers would love to have in abundance.

Swimmers may try to change their biological make-up through training (thinking that swimming a lot of sprints will change slow twitch fibers into fast twitch fibers). This cannot be done. An Olympic level 50 freestyler will not be able to win the Olympic 1500 or visa versa. One cannot train fast twitch to *be* slow twitch or the other way around. Swimmers can increase the size of the fast twitch muscle fibers they *do* have, or increase the endurance of their slow

Innovative Stretchcord Training for Swimmers

twitch fibers, (or either in their FOG fibers), but they cannot change fiber types from one to another.

Since most swimming events are short and require a great deal of strength and power, the goal of most resistance training programs is to strengthen the fast twitch muscle fibers. Probably 99% of all resistance training programs, including those with stretchcords, fall short of getting every fast twitch fiber. The reason lies within the way humans recruit their muscle fibers. When humans start to exercise, they use slow twitch muscle fibers only. As the work becomes more difficult, they activate FOG fibers, and then finally they use their fast twitch fibers as they near fatigue. They must reach fatigue to use every fast twitch fiber within a muscle. See the following graph.

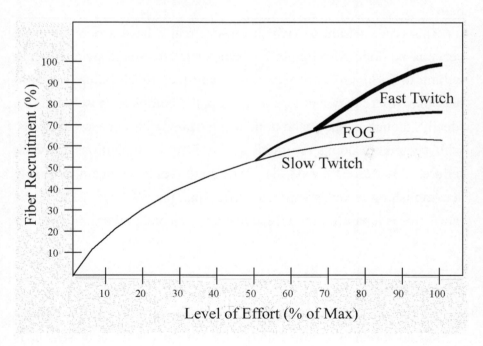

What this is saying is that if swimmers want to train their fast twitch muscles to have more power, they need to exercise

to fatigue on each set. Otherwise, they are not training every fast twitch fiber within the muscle. Many sets are only designed to task swimmers at 80 to 90 percent of their muscular force and therefore work very little fast twitch muscle.

There is nothing pleasant about training fast twitch muscle in this manner. It is very painful to take resistance sets to complete fatigue time after time, but it *is* the only way to train every fast twitch muscle in a body area. By doing so, one becomes significantly stronger than one would by only training to 80 percent. And by training every muscle—as opposed to only 80%--the strength gain will be worth the pain.

This type of training (which doesn't really have a popular name yet) *can* be done with lighter resistance stretchcords if swimmers are willing to do *hundreds* of repetitions until they reach failure or get to the point where they can't do another pull—complete muscle fatigue. Ideally, though, it should be done using heavy resistance stretchcords, with swimmers doing an initial set of 8 to 12 repetitions to reach failure. After a rest period, they will do the same set again, probably accomplishing fewer repetitions. After that, they'll do it again. Once more, this is a painful, but effective way to increase swimming power.

Periodization

Periodization is a term often used for how a training season is broken into phases, from getting-started (returning from vacation) to the big championship meet. It is important to understand the periods that constitute the swim program so that stretchcord training can be geared to complement them. In general, swimming programs go through these phases: 1) Base/Technique, 2) Endurance, 3) Race-Specific, 4) Taper, and 5) Rest/Recovery. Different coaches may have their own names and numbers, but they will likely follow this general outline.

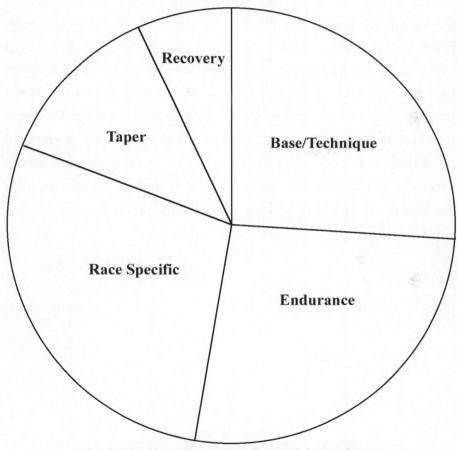

Periodization Through a Typical Swim Season

Stretchcord training doesn't have to mirror swim training, and in fact, probably shouldn't. For example, race-specific stretchcord work can begin in the Base/Technique period and last through the Race-Specific period. Some coaches might have their swimmers even do race-specific training during the off-season or during taper. The coach should be used as the guide for when to do what type of training. However, don't do base or endurance stretchcord training during the swimming taper phase as this will compromise needed rest. Normally, stretchcord training should be one phase or period ahead of the swimming phase. So, when a swimmer is not yet in the pool, prior to the season starting, they can be doing *base* stretchcord training. When they get into the pool and their team is working on base training, they can be doing *endurance* stretchcord work. When the swim team is doing race-specific training, that's when the *taper* (or fast explosive, higher resistance, less repetition) stretchcord training should occur. And finally, when the team is tapering, quick, explosive stretchcord training can occur, though more than likely a Rest/Recovery period should occur in stretchcord training.

THREE

CHILDREN AND STRETCHCORDS

"No weight training for children!" For years, we as a society have believed that weight lifting (or resistance training) is bad for kids. Ask a knowledgeable individual if children should do strength training and you're likely to hear, "No, it will stunt their growth." Some may even add, "Studies have shown that it will hinder their development." It is unclear where this idea originated, but it is a prevailing belief of many parents, coaches and educators. The truth is, resistance training has *never* been shown to stunt children's growth. This is a wives tale. *Appropriate* resistance training is good for healthy children.

The U.S. Olympic Committee has recently published research that states there is no evidence that strength training is detrimental to children or that it stunts their growth (Riewald & Cinea, 2003). When given some thought, this only makes sense. Swimming itself is strength/resistance training and children have been benefiting from swimming for years. Swimming is a resistance exercise against the water, and far from thinking it might stunt growth, we expect and in fact know from many years of experience, that it will *help* children grow.

The human body does not respond to stress by getting smaller and weaker. The body responds by getting bigger and stronger. This happens not only to the muscles of the body, but to the bones, tendons, cartilage and ligaments. Physical stress can create positive physical changes and swimming is a great example of this.

There is one caution that should be considered when children undergo dryland training. Children's bones are softer and more pliable than those of adolescents and adults. The bone-tendon attachments are not fully developed. In adults, exercise strengthens the bone-tendon junction as the muscle grows. This makes it so the muscle should never be able to create enough force to pull the tendon off the bone. In general, children don't make this adaptation at the same rate as adults. It is possible for their muscles to over-develop and pull their tendons from their bones. This is rare, but it is possible. To prevent this, *rapid* gains in strength for children should be avoided. Children should be placed on *long-term* strength gain programs.

How old is old enough to start a dryland stretchcord training program? In general, there is little need to start a child age 7 or under on dryland training, though there may be exceptions to this. If a parent is thinking about having their 7-year old child do a stretchcord program, they should consult their child's coach and physician before progressing. Frankly, the same should be done for a child of any age. The coach is the first and best resource for their swimmers and should oversee any dryland training. If a swimmer over-trains on stretchcords one morning and the coach has a long pull set during swim practice that afternoon, the risk of an overuse shoulder injury is greatly increased. So, before starting a stretchcord program, talk to your coach, and if there are any possibilities of shoulder problems, consult a sports medicine specialist as well.

In general, children ages 8 and up can do some kind of stretchcord training program. There are a number of reasons to recommend it. The biggest reason for younger children to train with stretchcords is time. Young children may not train swimming more than 3 times per week during the school year because of other activities (and the potential of future burnout). Stretchcord training can supplement swim training and be done in a short period of time. A young swimmer could *train* 5 to 7 days a week, but actually get into the pool only three of those days. Stretchcord training may be a simple five to ten-minute routine. Compare this to driving to the pool, swimming, showering and driving home. Now it is really worth the money to buy a set or two of stretchcords.

Here is a special note for parents who buy stretchcords for their swimmers. Some parents are bound and determined to have their swimmer be the best at any cost. Kids frequently grow to resent what they are forced to do. If the child wants to swim and be great at it, they will embrace stretchcord training to help them reach their goals and there are ways to make stretchcords fun. If they don't, be careful what you force upon them.

FOUR

HOW MUCH, HOW OFTEN

When starting a new strength gain program, training should begin slowly. Swimmers should start on stretchcords that are not too difficult for them (see Chapter One, Types of Stretchcords). If a swimmer can perform 25-50 butterfly pulls (double arm pulls) with a set of cords without stopping, then those cords are good start-up cords. If not, get easier cords. If a swimmer has never done stretchcord training before (many masters and older age-group swimmers have), then the focus should be on proper technique. This book is designed to help swimmers learn proper technique for all four strokes with the aim of directly transferring stretchcord training to swimming success. Once swimmers demonstrates they can perform proper technique, then they can begin actual stretchcord *training* in that stroke. This shouldn't take long, a few days to a week at most.

One of the good things about stretchcord training as opposed to swimming is simplicity. Stretchcord training does not require a breathing pattern (though one *can* be incorporated), it does not require rotation, and it does not require a synchronous kick. The only thing swimmers need concentrate on is their hand pull pattern. Once arm movements are proficient, swimmers can add rotation, breathing patterns and other race specific techniques.

Once the proper technique is mastered, swimmers can spend between 5 and 30 minutes a day doing stretchcord exercises. Exercises can be broken into more than one session. The amount swimmers perform depends on their physical maturity, current swim yardage, the time of the season and other factors. As always, the coach is the best resource for any questions. Stretchcords can help almost any swimmer. They can add strength and endurance to athletes who are swimming six days a week. They can act like another practice for swimmers who want to train twice a day but can only make it to the pool once a day. They can keep swimmers in shape during the off-season. And they can help swimmers prepare for specific races.

The best place to start when wondering how much to do is to ask your coach. Most coaches like their swimmers to do dryland training and if the swimmers do it at home, that leaves more time for swimming when they come to the pool. If enough swimmers on a team have stretchcords at home, then coaches can design specific workouts for their groups for specific days. This makes the most of water time for all swimmers.

Without the aide of a coach, (for some age-group swimmers, several triathletes and many masters swimmers) here are some good guidelines to follow when incorporating a stretchcord program into your training. Like swimming, stretchcord exercises can be done every day, but the body will probably perform better with at least one day of rest per week. If swimmers are doing a lot of exercises repetitions with heavy resistance stretchcords (say the maximum number of butterfly pulls they can do is 20), and they work until failure several times during a workout, then taking a day of rest after every one or two days is recommended.

In general, time may not be a good way to judge a stretchcord workout. If high resistance stretchcords are being used, more rest between sets will be needed. However, setting a workout time *can* provide a workload estimation. If swimmers are swimming twice a day, then there is already a lot of stress on their bodies. Additional training *could* make them perform better. But it could also worsen their performance, or cause injury. Careful monitoring is required. Swimmers and coaches need to team together to best plan for peak performances and injury prevention. This means that swimmers need to communicate with their coaches on a regular basis about how they feel, if they're getting tired or sore, or feel strong. Coaches can then adjust both stretchcord and swim workouts accordingly.

Ten to 30 minutes of training is a good amount for swimmers who are swimming once a day. This assumes that once-a-day training is not completely exhausting. Swimmers will need to evaluate what is best for them based on trial and error. For some swimmers, five minutes is the right amount. This may include younger swimmers. Other swimmers may perform better with significantly more stretchcord training.

For swimmers not swimming, during the off-season, 30 plus minutes of stretchcord training can be done. Again, this may or may not take place in a single session. Swimmers can train twice a day for 15 minutes or 3 times for 10 minutes. In the long run, the minutes won't really matter, but what is done during those minutes will.

There are no studies on the ideal daily or weekly amount of stretchcord training swimmers should do. Each swimmer is unique, and any guidelines that are developed will not fit everyone. For motivated swimmers who just want to count the number of pulls they perform, the following chart can be used as a guideline. Swimmers who can perform 50 to 100 pulls with a specific stretchcord should not exceed the following on a daily or weekly basis.

Age	Max # of Pulls/day	Max # of Pulls/week	Time
8-10	300*	1500	10 min
11-13	500*	2500	15 Min
14 & older	800*	4000	20 Min

*Based on a swimmer who can perform between 50 and 100 pulls in a row with specific stretchcords. As no studies have been done on stretchcord use, these guidelines have been set based on the author's experience. Pulls are both left and right arms (cycles). "Time" is the actual time spent pulling, not including rest periods.

The above table indicates that an intensive stretchcord training program for a 13-year old who can do 75 pulls in a row with a set of stretchcords should probably not include more than 500 total pulls in one day. This may mean 10 x 50 pulls, spread out during the day (probably not all in one session). It might mean 4 x 50 before school and another 4 x 50 right after school and then 2 x 50 before bed. This book will not recommend more than 2500 pulls over a weeks' time, which at the above rate would be 5 days of 500 pulls with 2 rest days. However, each individual is different and there may be some who perform better with higher workloads. If a swimmer wants to do more pulls and a coach agrees that more could benefit them, it can be given a go to find out if better swimming results.

Here is a quick warning about these numbers. They are written to be *maximum* numbers, not *optimum* numbers. Athletes' needs differ from individual to individual. Joe Swimmer would probably be wrong to think that just because he is 14, he won't swim fast unless he performs 800 pulls a day. 95% of all swimmers will probably perform better with less than 800 pulls a day. Go back and review the overload principal as well as overtraining and then give the body time to recover. Over*load* is good, but over*training* will not lead to better swimming times.

FIVE

USING STRETCHCORDS

Already mentioned was that stretchcords could be used to specifically train all four strokes. Undoubtedly, this has left several readers wondering how in the world stretchcords could be used to mimic *back*stroke. Normally stretchcords are tied to some post or pole and the swimmer bends forward at the waist and pulls (pictured). In this set-up, swimmers can rather easily perform a butterfly, freestyle or breaststroke-type of pull. Since swimmers cannot bend over backwards at the waist like they can forward when standing up, backstroke cannot be mimicked with cords set up in this manner. Perhaps 95% of all stretchcord training is done this way. Swimmers have probably done resistance band training this way for 40 years because it seems to be more like swimming, the upper body being horizontal.

To allow for backstroke-like pulling and body rotation, however, another way to use stretchcords is to hang them from above. This can be done from the ceiling, a deck, the house eaves, a tree branch, or anything that is around 4 meters (13 feet) high or higher. The height of the stretchcords is good when swimmers have to jump up to grasp them. If a swimmer cannot jump up and reach the handles/paddles, then the stretchcords should be lowered some. In situations where the stretchcords are hung too high (because the ceiling or branch is too high), an extension can be added to the stretchcords, such as a piece of rope, to make the stretchcords hang at the right height.

Using stretchcords that are hung from above can be more comfortable for swimmers because they don't have to bend over. Anytime athletes are more comfortable, two things are likely to happen. The first is they will do a better job on their exercises. The second is that they are more likely to exercise again. Stretchcords hung from above can also provide better work, because gravity helps hold the swimmer away from the tie-off point. And, of course, backstroke becomes possible during stretchcord training when cords are hung from above.

Most homes or pools offer something that will allow swimmers to use stretchcords hung from above. Here are some words of advice that should be read a few times and taken very seriously.

Wherever the stretchcords are tied off, whether from above or in front of the swimmer, they must be *solidly* secured.

This is critical. Picture this ugly scene. A stretchcord is fastened to a stair banister. A swimmer starts pulling and after 100 pulls, the banister breaks, and a large hunk of wood or metal comes flying (literally shot out of a sling shot) towards the swimmer's head. Not pretty! So, make sure whatever the stretchcord is attached to can hold the weight of *three* swimmers and is rock solid. Once this is assured, safe stretchcord training can begin.

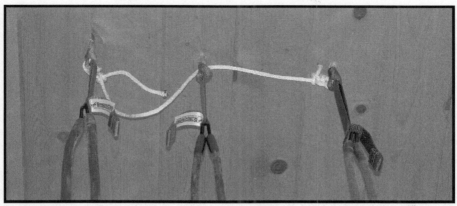

Here is a series of three StrechCordz®, each attached to ceiling joists via I-bolts. Each I-bolt is secured to the others so that if one comes undone, the other two will stop the stretchcord and bolt from shooting towards the user.

Hanging stretchcords from the ceiling makes doing other strokes easier. In the past nearly all stretchcord exercises were done with a double arm, butterfly-like, arm pull. There are several reasons for this. First and foremost, the butterfly pull is a very efficient way to accomplish a lot of pulls. It is also a very simple movement to complete without complex timing or rotation. Additionally, it probably develops the greatest overall strength per minute of exercise. As freestyle in the pool is the predominant stroke, the butterfly pull in stretchcord training should be considered predominant. Depending on one's goals, most stretchcord work should be done using the butterfly motion. This is especially true for freestyle, as the butterfly pull pattern is very similar to freestyle. Breaststroke and backstroke have slightly different pull patterns, which not only activate different muscles, but also activate muscles from different positions. For these reasons, and because it reduces boredom to add variety to dryland training, all four strokes will be presented in this book.

Strokes on Stretchcords

It is very important to perform stretchcord exercises just as one *should* perform the stroke in the water. This is because, remember, *what is practiced on land will find its way into the water*, both good and bad. Each pull should emphasize correct hand movement patterns with high elbows. The upcoming sections highlight the correct way to perform stretchcord training in each stroke, with pictures for illustration.

Great care has been taken to insure that the illustrations in this book display proper technique, not only for increasing power in the water, but also for reducing drag. So it is very important that swimmers mimic the illustrations. Many swimmers *believe* they are performing a movement correctly, when in fact they are not. Coaches all over the world can attest to this. The perception of where their arms are in the water (or in the air when it comes to stretchcord training) and their arms' actual locations do not *sync*. This is why it is recommended that someone (preferably a coach) monitor stretchcord training until perfect pull patterns become habit. In addition, having a mirror placed where swimmers can monitor *themselves* is a helpful tool. If no one is available to do the former, swimmers can use a video camera and periodically check themselves for needed corrections. This can also be fun. They may be surprised. *Practice doesn't make perfect, it makes permanent.*

SIX

STRETCHCORD SWIMMING

Butterfly

Recall that the butterfly pull pattern should be the primary stretchcord exercise because it is an efficient way to perform the most work in the least amount of time. In the butterfly stretchcord pull, the hands reach towards the band attachment location to extend the shoulder joints. The hands then start the pull, moving toward the face with the thumbs about hand-width apart. During this movement, *the elbows should remain in position above the head.*

Butterfly pull (head on). 1) Start in the streamline position. 2) Good high elbows. 3) Keep hands within the body's width. 4) Push all the way through full arm extension.

Once the hands reach the level of the elbows (either on the pull or the recovery), the elbows and upper arms will follow. During the pull, wrists should be forward (fingers forward if done with paddles), away from the swimmer, thumbs directed at each other. The elbows should be fully extended at the finish of the pull past the hips, and the arms should recover behind the back with elbows bent.

Some swimmers may not be able to recover with arms behind the back and elbows bent because they lack shoulder flexibility. Chances are extremely high that lack of shoulder flexibility is hurting their butterfly stroke. Swimmers who lack shoulder flexibility find butterfly recovery to be very hard work. This limits the time they can maintain their butterfly speed in the water. Many times, these swimmers can muscle through a good 50 fly, but not a 100 or a 200. Long course races exacerbate their problem. Stretchcord butterfly can help swimmers' recovery flexibility. Swimmers who struggle with the butterfly recovery should try keeping their elbows as "high" (far back) as possible during stretchcord recovery. Slowly, but surely, flexibility will increase.

Another way to recover is to move the arms directly back along the pull path (keeping the elbows high). This is a good change-up for any exercise, because the same muscles responsible for *pulling* are responsible for slowing the hand movements *down* in such a reverse exercise. These are *eccentric* muscle contractions, and eccentric work can lead to increased power during the swimming pull phase. Because of this, recovery can and perhaps should be done this way about every *other* session, perhaps a week of normal and a week of what we'll call "eccentric reverse recovery".

If shoulder flexibility is not an issue when swimming butterfly, then eccentric reverse recovery can be done about every other session

Innovative Stretchcord Training for Swimmers

or week. If flexibility *is* an issue, then high elbow/behind the back recovery should be used to help increase flexibility. One note here, increasing flexibility, and stretchcord work for that matter, can make the joints sore. Sore *muscles* (tenderness/soreness along the lines of muscles) are okay and will recover with aerobic training or rest. Sore *joints* (spot soreness on joints) need rest.

Butterfly pull (side). 1) Streamline start. 2) At the catch of the butterfly pull, the wrists flex while the elbows stay high. 3) Hands pull the cords down while elbows remain high. 4) Press through until the elbows are locked on either side of the hips. 5) In the recovery phase, hands should come back up to the start position behind the back. 6) Elbows should remain bent and high throughout the recovery and behind the back as much as possible.

Backstroke

It is recommended that backstroke be done with stretchcords fastened above the swimmer. Backstroke can also be performed with the cords tied off a meter above the ground if a swimmer is lying face-up on a bench. Benches usually don't allow the easy side-to-side rotation that standing does. If a swimmer has no way to tie stretchcords overhead, then lying on a bench is the next best option.

As with all strokes, backstroke stretchcord pulls should start from a streamline position. The hands should be overhead, one on top of the other with straight elbows. The anterior (front) muscles of the upper arms, the biceps should be squeezed against the ears. Also, as with the other strokes, the first thing that should move in the backstroke pull is the hand. The wrist should flex for the backstroke "catch". Then, as the hand pulls towards the lower body, the elbow should begin to move behind the plane of the back (the body will rotate to the side). The elbow should remain in position (above the head) until the hand comes level with or passes it. Just as in butterfly, this should happen near the top of the head. Then, as the hand continues to move, it will pull the elbow and upper arm along with it. During both the backstroke pull and recovery, the head should remain still, not rotate side to side with the body. Position checks can be made instantly with a mirror on the wall in front of the swimmer.

To recover, swimmers can do just what they do during the actual backstroke—bring their arms up in front of their bodies, elbows straight. If the swimmer is standing up, they should rotate at the hips to help both their recovery and their pull.

Innovative Stretchcord Training for Swimmers

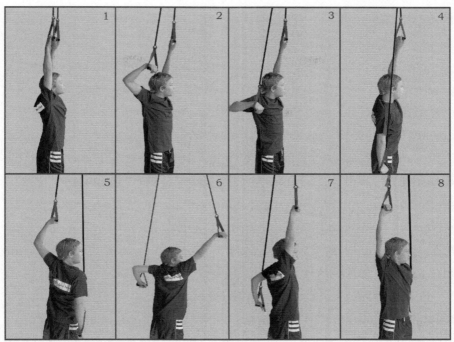

Backstroke pull (side) with traditional recovery. 1) Start in the backstroke streamline position. 2) High elbow catch and body rotation towards pulling arm. 3) Pull down the side of the body remaining in rotation. 4) Finish all the way through. 5) Left arm in good catch position as body rotates the other direction and right arm begins to recover. 6) Good body rotation and deep pulling position with left arm. 7) Deep pulling position remains as body rotates back towards center. 8) Left arm completes pull, body rotates and right arm is ready for catch position.

Or again, swimmers can recover retracing their backstroke pull patterns. This can take a bit of practice, as it seems to be less natural than when retracing the butterfly pattern. But again, these *eccentric* muscle contractions can be highly beneficial, so eccentric reverse recovery warrants practice on a regular basis.

Alan W. Arata

Breaststroke

The breaststroke hand pull pattern can be approximated using a single set of stretchcords. The muscle activation pattern is a bit different, since in swimming, the hands tend to move at angles that are not always directly opposite of where the stretchcords put them. Still, stretchcords can provide good resistance for most of the breaststroke pull pattern, especially in the very important "catch" section of the pull. To *better* approximate the breaststroke pull, a *system* of cords can be used to provide resistance throughout the pull. NZ MFG has a StrechCordz® designed specifically for the breaststroke pull pattern.

Breaststroke stretchcord work should be done starting in the extended position, both hands at their closest point to the stretchcord's attachment. The beginning or "catch" phase of the breaststroke pull looks nearly identical to that of butterfly. After the catch in breaststroke, however, the hands move *wider* than the shoulders—elbows still remaining as high as possible. Once the hands are at shoulder level and even with or below the elbows, the pull continues down but *inward* towards the bellybutton. Some swimmers may say that they don't swim breaststroke pulling all the way to their bellybuttons, and think, *Why do stretchcords that far down?* In fact, most swimmers *don't* pull that far. However, by pulling a little beyond the range of motion as compared to the normal stroke pattern, additional strength can be gained to help swimmers finish off their strokes when they feel tired. *Note: this is not possible in the other strokes since the stroke finish is also the limit of arm extension.*

Breaststroke recovery can be performed with the hands together moving directly up the centerline. Unlike the other strokes, this time

Innovative Stretchcord Training for Swimmers

the hands lead and the elbows follow. It is also a good idea for swimmers to keep their hands as close to their chests as possible during recovery. In the water, the closer to the chest (or even somewhat out of the water), the less drag.

Breaststroke pull (head on) using specially designed Breaststroke StrechCordz®. 1) Streamline position. 2) High elbow, strong catch position. 3) Elbows make a right angle during the pull with elbows high. 4) Hands go down to the waist—this may be further than most breaststrokers pull, but by working beyond the normal breaststroke range, swimmers should be able to generate more power at the end of their pull patterns. 5) Hands move to centerline of body to begin recovery. 6) Hands and elbows recover up the centerline of the body.

Alan W. Arata

Breaststroke pull (side). 1) Streamline position. 2) Catch with the hands moving first, elbows high. 3) High Elbow position with a 90° elbow bend. 4) Press through. 5) Finish down by the waist. 6) Hands recover up the center of the body.

Eccentric reverse recovery can be performed during stretchcord breaststroke as well. As in backstroke, it is not as natural as a stroke-like recovery, but is worth using on a rotating basis for the eccentric benefit.

Freestyle

The freestyle stroke starts with both shoulders and both elbows fully extended in the streamline position. Again, the first thing that should move is a hand. Swimmers should start with the hand that moves first when they swim. The hand moves while the elbow remains high and in place as long as possible. The body should rotate towards the right if the right hand is pulling and towards the left if the left hand is pulling. This rotation is more easily accomplished when cords are attached above, as can be seen in one of the examples of freestyle pulling shown.

The hand follows a path that takes it centrally down the body, nose to midsection, about 12 inches (.3 meters) in front of the body, before finishing at around mid-thigh level. To say it another way, as the hand starts its movement, the elbow will start to bend, but the upper arm (shoulder to elbow) should remain in place until the hand is on level with or below/behind the elbow. The hand should reach this position at about head level. From there, the hand continues down the centerline of the body with the elbow and upper arm following (high elbows). At the end of the pull motion, as the elbow is nearing full extension, the hand sweeps past the thigh to complete the power phase of the pull cycle. As the hand moves past the thigh in preparation for the recovery phase, the body should/will rotate to the other side. Stretchcords attached from above greatly facilitate this rotation.

Alan W. Arata

The catch position in freestyle stretchcord work (bottom) looks very much like the catch position in freestyle swimming (top).

To recover, the hands can move up the swimmers' sides, thumbs skimming the sides of the body, elbows bent. For this recovery pattern, swimmers' elbows should remain above/in front of the hands until the hands reach the shoulders, at which time the hands move in front of the elbows. Hands continue towards the tie-off point until the elbows are fully extended again. This completes the freestyle recovery the way it should be done while swimming. There are swimmers who use more of a windmill-like recovery during freestyle. This is not recommended when using stretchcords because of injury potential. The shortest distance between two points *is* a straight line and the hand can only follow a straight line-like path if the elbow is *bent*.

Innovative Stretchcord Training for Swimmers

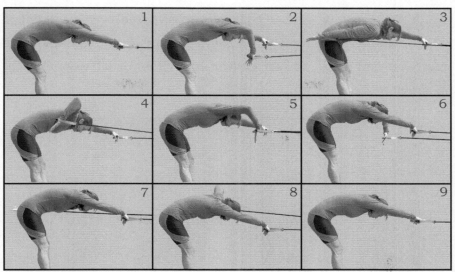

Horizontal freestyle stretchcord training (side). 1) Start in the streamline position. 2) High elbow catch. 3) Finish to the very extent of the arm's reach. 4) Recover mimicking an in-the-water fingertip drag drill. 5) Keep elbow high through recovery. 6) High elbow catch with the left hand. 7) Finish to the very extent of the arm's reach. 8) Left hand recovers with fingertip drag-like drill. 9) A full catch-up position and the right hand is ready to begin the next stroke cycle.

Here is another important thing about doing freestyle with stretchcords. It can be difficult to keep the arms 180° apart when exercising (one pulling while the other is recovering). Many swimmers swim this way, and that's fine. However, the stretchcord freestyle is probably best done using a "catch-up" stroke where the hands meet at the top (closest to the tie-off point) before the next arm-pull begins. This will keep the stroke pattern consistent and help swimmers with correct high-elbow position. It may also lead a swimmer to do more of a catch-up stroke in the water. The high elbow position aids in power production. Remember, there are only

Alan W. Arata

two things that a swimmer can do to increase speed—reduce drag and produce more power. This is perhaps why most Olympic men freestylers and many women use some variation of a freestyle catch-up stroke.

Standing freestyle stretchcord training (head on). 1) Start in the streamline position. 2) Good high elbow catch position. 3) Pushing through with hand in proper position. 4) Finish the pull past the hip. 5) Recover by maintaining the high elbow position and rotate to opposite side. 6) Catch position with the opposite hand. 7) Finish the pull past the hips. 8) Rotate during recovery and begin the next stroke cycle.

Varying the Resistance

There will be days when swimmers and coaches will want more resistance from stretchcord training. This may be because the swimmers have grown stronger and need increased resistance on a daily basis to keep progressing—the Overload Principle—or, they might want to spend some time doing more sprint-like training, or just to do a set of pulls at a higher resistance to test themselves. Whatever the reason, there are several ways to vary the resistance of a stretchcord training session. The best (and safest) way is to purchase the next thickness level or heavier resistance stretchcord. If swimmers need to increase resistance regularly, then a new set of higher tension stretchcords is the way to go.

When swimmers want to increase resistance for only a training session or even a week of training sessions, then there is a simple way using the stretchcords they already possess. If swimmers have the stretchcord tied off at waist height, doing the pulls from the horizontal position, they can increase their resistance by simply moving further from the tie-off point. It is recommended that swimmers using this technique place tape (or some kind of semi-permanent mark) on the floor to indicate their foot placement in order to train at a consistent level each day.

Swimmers who use stretchcords fastened from above cannot simply back away. If the cords can be raised, this is an easy fix—raise the stretchcords to increase the resistance. If the cords cannot be raised, swimmers can kneel to increase the tension. Kneeling on a small stool may be a good intermediate position. Kneeling on the floor will offer even more resistance.

I highly recommend that swimmers use different levels of stretchcords for different workouts rather than stretching easy cords to new lengths. Stretchcords are not expensive. It may cost around $100 USD to buy *three* levels of good stretchcords. Swimming parents often spend more than this on entry fees for their swimmers for just one State Championship meet. If someone is willing to spend that on entry fees, they should be willing to spend it on something that will help their swimmers do better in *all* their meets.

SEVEN

OTHER STRETCHCORD EXERCISES

All and all, stretchcords are very useful and versatile pieces of exercise equipment and they can do more for swimmers than mimic a swimming pull pattern. Handled stretchcords can isolate wrist muscles to strengthen a swimmer's "grip" on the water. Stretchcords can be used for *leg* exercises, which may translate into a better, stronger kick. All of these things are good for swimmers, meaning more can be done with stretchcords to help swimming speed than just mimicking a swimming pull pattern.

Additionally, physical therapists have been using resistance bands for years to rehabilitate, among other things, the shoulders of swimmers. If swimmers don't *have* shoulder injuries, stretchcords can be used to help keep them injury free. So stretchcords are good for injury prevention and rehab, as well as for endurance and power development.

Forearm Muscles Workout

The forearm or wrist muscles are often an overlooked muscle group in swimming exercise programs. If the forearm muscles fatigue, then the hand cannot maintain the optimum position to create propulsion. When wrist muscles fatigue, then no matter how much strength is left in the core, back and arm muscles, swimmers will not be able to gain optimum leverage on the water. In swimming this is called slipping. Pretty much every swimmer has felt it during a race or practice. Strengthening the muscles of the forearms will help prevent or as a minimum delay this feeling.

Handled stretchcords can provide a quick and simple way to work the forearm muscles. Stand on the stretchcords with elbows at the sides bent to 90°, grasp the handles and roll the hands from *wrist extension* to *wrist flexion* as seen below. If the stretchcords are attached above, the reverse can be done, rolling the hands downward. This process can continue until the forearm muscles are completely fatigued, usually somewhere up to a minute. If it takes longer, more resistance is needed. Afterwards, writing, typing and other tasks that take manual dexterity will be difficult until the muscles loosen up and recover.

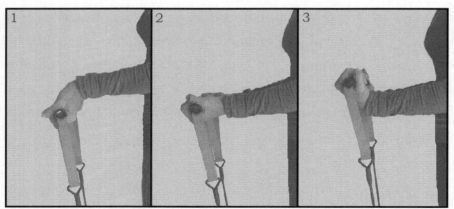

Forearm strengthening. 1) Start in complete wrist extension. 2) Maintain firm grip on the handles. 3) Finish in complete wrist flexion.

The Catch

Many swim coaches think the catch is the most important phase of the swimming stroke. The catch is what establishes swimmers' ability to provide upper body propulsion. The earlier the catch, the longer the swimmer will be able to apply force and the faster they will go. Stretchcords can work the catch position to near perfection.

The key to perform the proper catch exercise is elbow movement, or lack thereof. The ideal catch has little to no elbow movement, as only the hands and forearms move.

The "catch" exercise. 1) Start in the streamline position. 2) Keep the elbows above/in front of the head, pull the stretchcords until the hands are at the top of the head.

Leg Workouts

Jumping-type leg strength is used for starts and turns in swimming. The more power the legs are capable of producing, the faster speeds a swimmer can obtain off of starts and turns. These are the parts of the race where a swimmer generates the greatest speed.

One of the best ways to increase jumping leg strength is through squat training. This can be done without having a big weight machine.

Squats

Leg squats can be done with stretchcords providing the resistance. Stand on the stretchcord tubing, feet about shoulder width apart, grasp the handles/paddles, bend the elbows, and stabilize the hands against the shoulders (picture below). Then perform squatting movements, keeping the back straight. In general, the leg muscles are much stronger than the arm muscles. Although returning to the standing position means overcoming both the swimmer's body weight and stretchcord resistance, heavy stretchcords are needed. Unlike stretchcord arm training that is designed to match the multiple continuous arm pulls needed when swimming in the water, squat training does not need to match multiple continuous leg motions. A start occurs just once during a race, and turns, even in a short course pool, happen no sooner than 10 seconds apart. So lower repetitions with high resistance and explosive movement should be used in squat exercises.

Squats with stretchcords are a great way to build up leg strength needed for explosive movements off both starts and turns.

When starts and turns do occur, swimmers should use all their force to leave the blocks or the wall. This is an explosive movement that requires a lot of force. For this reason squat *exercises* should also be quick and explosive (just 6 to 10 reps). Bigger, stronger swimmers may need to use two stretchcord bands simultaneously to provide enough resistance for such exercises.

Groin Work

Other leg workouts can also be accomplished with stretchcords. Strained groin muscles can sideline breaststrokers for prolonged periods of time. To strengthen the groin muscles, a swimmer should attach the tie-off point of their stretchcord to a fixed object at around ankle level and the other end to one of their ankles. StrechCordz® (www.nzmfg.com) makes special ankle attachments that can aide in this exercise. Standing sideways away from the wall so the cord is just taut and the attached leg is nearest the wall, move the leg past the centerline of the body across the other as pictured.

It is very important not to overdo this exercise during the first few sessions. If swimmers use too high a resistance or do too many repetitions, they may aggravate the groin muscle. Another possibility is that they may tire the groin and then pull or strain the muscle in subsequent swim practice. Since neither of these is desired, one should start with few repetitions and light stretchcords and build up strength over a period of months, not days or even weeks.

The opposite motion (hip abduction) is also important for breaststrokers, not so much to prevent injury, but to provide strength to get the legs in the proper kicking position. These thigh abduction muscles are not highly used in other swimming strokes or in most human activities. If the muscles tire, which can easily happen during an all-out race, the force produced by the kick can fade quickly.

The thigh abduction exercise is simply the opposite of the groin exercise above and can be done with the same cords. Swimmers should shift the cuffs on their legs and turn around. The exercise is done by moving the cord-attached leg to the side, *away* for the other leg. With both exercises, it is often helpful to have something to hold on to for balance.

As with most exercises, one should start slowly, especially when working the groin muscles, using light resistance. Significantly *overdeveloping* either the groin muscles or the abductors will not increase swimming speed. The exercises are simply to *strengthen* the areas if they are weak. This can enable breaststroke kick training to be done without injury.

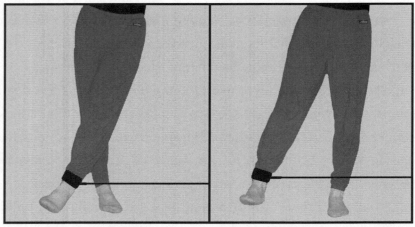

Leg adduction (left) and abduction (right) help strengthen muscles that are critical for breaststroke. Just turn around to work both sets of muscles, then change the strap to the other leg.

Kicking

Flutter and dolphin kicking can also be mimicked with stretchcords, though really not very well. In fact, no effective out-of-water kicking aid really exists to date. But if a swimmer were unable to enter the water for a few weeks, a stretchcord kick program *could* be set up. For this purpose, attach the cords to something low, like the legs of some heavy furniture. Attach the straps to the ankles and lie supine (face up) on a platform (could be some furniture) and perform a flutter or dolphin kick-like motion. After a certain number of repetitions, turn over and repeat the exercise on the stomach. This will work both the fronts and the backs of the legs, upstroke and downstroke of the kick. The water, however, is by far the better place to work the legs for flutter and dolphin kicking.

Breaststroke kicking can more *easily* be mimicked out of the water with stretchcords than the other kicks. In addition, working on the whip kick using stretchcords can increase swimmers hip, knee and foot flexibility in the swimming movement. This can greatly increase breaststroke kicking power and speed. Place the feet through the handles/paddles or use the specially made ankle StrechCordz® and place the ankle band around the arch on the foot. The cords themselves can be held in the swimmers' hands, bands against the shoulders. Swimmers then lie or sit on a bench, stool, or the side of a couch on either their stomachs or backs. If on their stomachs, they must be able to bend their hips to 90° and not touch the floor. From their fronts or backs, swimmers should be able to perform the breaststroke kick, with a very similar motion to what they use in the water, using stretchcords as resistance.

Alan W. Arata

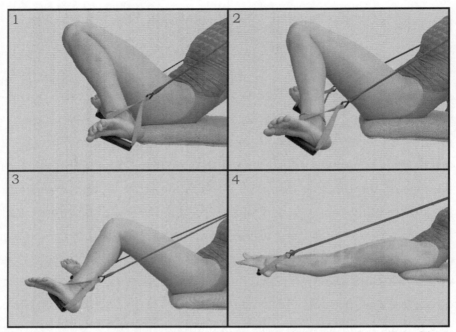

The breaststroke kick can be mimicked with stretchcords. Since the legs are quite strong, high resistance cords should be used. 1) Start with heels on the outside of the buttocks. 2) Push using the heels and the insides of the feet. 3) The knees should remain about fist-width apart during the kicking motion. 4) Finish with full extension of the legs and pointed toes.

It is important to perform the movement correctly. Hip angle (trunk to upper leg angle) should be between 100 and 120°. The knees should be from fist-width to shoulder-width apart (fist-width will help increase breaststroke kick flexibility). Whether using handles or paddles for this exercise, the pressure on the attaching apparatus should come from the heels as it would in the water. Kicking motions should be finished with pointed toes (picture 4).

Increased breaststroke kick flexibility is one of the benefits to doing the exercise, especially for those who lack the flexibility to perform a proper breaststroke kick to its optimum. But, because of the extended stretch, there is an increased risk of joint soreness. Sore joints need rest, so if soreness occurs, proceed slowly or take time off that exercise before starting back slowly.

Injury Prevention/Rehabilitation

Better than rehabilitating a shoulder is preventing a shoulder injury from occurring in the first place. Shoulder injuries in swimmers are usually caused by overuse and/or improper muscle balance. Often, these injuries occur in the rotator cuff muscles. Many shoulder injuries can be prevented with just a few minutes of light rotator cuff work each day. And swimmers who already have shoulder injuries can rehabilitate them through rotator cuff work. For these exercises use a stretchcord band with light resistance.

Rotator cuff muscles provide stability to the shoulder. There are three simple exercises that can be used to strengthen these muscles. The first is *internal rotation of the shoulder*. Position the arm by letting it hang down directly below the shoulder with the elbow bent at 90 degrees, hand out to the side (picture 1 below). The stretchcord should be attached to an object at about elbow height. The hand then pulls the cord towards the stomach while the elbow stays at 90 degrees against the body. This exercise should be repeated with a very light resistance, 25 to 50 times.

External rotation is the opposite of internal rotation. For this exercise, the arm again hangs down directly beneath the shoulder with the elbow bent at 90 degrees, but with the arm across the stomach (picture 4 below). The hand pulls the stretchcord back, *away* from the body. Light stretchcord resistance should be used for 25 to 50 pulls.

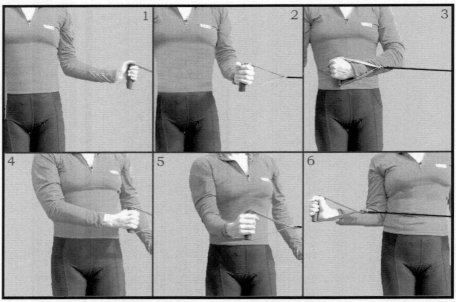

Rotator cuff exercise—1-3 internal rotation, 4-6 external rotation.

The last rotator cuff exercise is *abduction of the shoulder*. For this exercise, detach the stretchcords and *stand* on them with arms hanging down directly below the shoulders (picture 1 below). Cross the stretchcords and raise one or both arm(s) out to the side, keeping the elbow(s) straight. Handles are not needed for rotator cuff exercises; they can all be done by grabbing a piece of medical tubing, though a set of lightweight stretchcords not only makes the exercise simple to set up but also makes it consistent from time to time.

Innovative Stretchcord Training for Swimmers

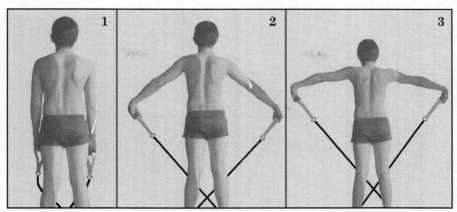

Rotator cuff exercise—shoulder abduction. Shoulder abduction exercises will not only strengthen the rotator cuff but can also aid the recovery stroke in butterfly. 1) Start in the resting position with the cords close to taught. 2) Keep elbows locked as hands and arms move out from the body. 3) Finish with the arms approximately parallel to the ground.

EIGHT

DESIGNING WORKOUTS

Training with stretchcords can be very flexible. Almost every swimming set done in the water can also be practiced on land. Stretchcord workouts can be as simple as 15 pulls (of any stroke), to something as complex as 10 x 100 IM on 1:30 with specific tempos and breathing patterns. The choice of difficulty and complexity is up to the swimmer.

Warm-up exercises can and should be done prior to serious swim-specific stretchcord training. A warm-up period is a great time to perform some of the other stretchcord exercises presented in the previous chapter. Internal and external shoulder rotation not only warms up the shoulders, but also helps prevent shoulder injuries. So, these exercises are a great way to start each training session—twenty-five pulls with each arm in both internal and external rotation with light stretchcords. After this, stroke-specific training can begin and can be interspersed with non-stroke exercises such as breaststroke kick, squats, etc.

Swimmers initially starting stretchcord stroke training should start simply and progress to more complicated sets. There will be some experienced swimmers who want to "get right on it," believing they can crank out some hard stretchcord workouts immediately. This is not recommend for two good reasons. The first concern is technique. A gradual start will allow swimmers to perfect their form while a rapid start will likely result in poor form. The second is time. Swimmers starting stretchcord training should do so with plenty of time prior to a big shave and taper meet. There should be time to start slowly. Swimming careers will last for years after the first stretchcord workout. There *is* time to take it slow and learn to do it right.

The first stretchcord training week should be used to perfect and concentrate on proper technique, swimmers performing no more than 15 repetitions with fairly light resistance. Video can be taken of the swimmer performing the exercises. Played back and paused in key places (or frame by frame advanced), these videos can be compared to the pictures in this book to help swimmers see whether they're performing the exercises correctly. A strategically placed mirror can allow self-corrections. Mirrors give real-time information, though action can't be stopped and broken down frame by frame as with video—both are good resources.

Since the butterfly pull pattern is the staple of stretchcord pulling, it should probably be perfected before any of the other strokes. In the following workout, four sets of butterfly pulls are done, each followed by 30 seconds rest. So, internal and external shoulder rotations for warm-up, then 15 butterfly pulls, 30 seconds rest, 12 butterfly pulls, an additional exercise like breaststroke kick or squats, 10 butterfly pulls, 30 seconds rest, 8 butterfly pulls, then some shoulder abductions and wrist curls to finish. This entire workout would take less than ten minutes with only around a minute of it being actual stretchcord pulling.

Monday	Morning	Evening
Internal Rotation	25 each	25 each
External Rotation	25 each	25 each
Fly	15	15
Fly	12	12
Breaststroke Kick	20	20
Fly	10	10
Fly	8	8
Shoulder Abduction	10	10
Wrist Curls	20	20

Each butterfly pull starts and ends with the hands above/in front of the head, elbows fully extended. This is the streamline position (and should be used to start all stretchcord pulling). The workouts should be written down to keep track of progress, and after each set is completed, the numbers can be scratched out:

Monday	Morning	Evening
Internal Rotation	~~25 each~~	~~25 each~~
External Rotation	~~25 each~~	~~25 each~~
Fly	~~15~~	~~15~~
Fly	~~12~~	~~12~~
Breaststroke Kick	~~20~~	~~20~~
Fly	~~10~~	~~10~~
Fly	~~8~~	~~8~~
Shoulder Abduction	~~10~~	~~10~~
Wrist Curls	~~20~~	~~20~~

Once the butterfly is perfected, other strokes can be added. The following is an example of an all stroke workout for a new puller:

Innovative Stretchcord Training for Swimmers

Monday	Morning	Evening
Internal Rotation	25 each	25 each
External Rotation	25 each	25 each
Fly	25	25
Back	15	15
Squats	20	20
Breast	15	15
Free	15	15
Leg ad/abduction	20	20
Shoulder Abduction	10	10
Butterfly Catch	20	20

Again, the workout should start with a warm-up of internal and external shoulder rotations, followed by more intensive exercises. Each stroke pull starts and ends with the hands above/in front of the head, elbows extended (the streamline position). Backstroke and freestyle pulls are complete cycles—right arm pull followed by left arm pull counts as one cycle. Other sets can be added to fit swimmers needs, such as squat work. After each set is completed, the numbers can be scratched out.

Once a routine has been followed for a week, the numbers can be increased. In resistance training, it is traditionally recommended to increase by about 10% per week. As this initial week is for form purposes as opposed to workout purposes, however, the second week can be notched up to 20 cycles all around. This would not generally include the internal or external shoulder rotations, as they are simple warm-up/injury prevention exercises. With the other exercises, however, use a video camera or have someone monitor the swimmer from time to time to insure proper form during every effort. Place a mirror so swimmers can monitor themselves. After the second week, swimmers can then move on to stretchcord *workouts*.

Another way to intensify training is to increase the number of *sets* (as opposed to repetitions *in* a set). In the following weeks, the routine might be *2* sets of 25. Later it can be 3 x 25 and then 4 x 25. It would not be unheard of to get to a point where one does 4 x 100 pulls of a stroke, squats or kicks. This becomes strenuous training, which should enhance swimming speed and endurance in the water.

Exercise can also be broken up between morning and evening. In the morning, one may work on butterfly and backstroke, while in the evening breaststroke and freestyle are the pull patterns. In addition, varying amounts of each type of pull can be done to best suit the swimmer. The stroke training part of the workout sheet for this might resemble the following.

Monday	Morning	Evening
Fly	3 x 40	
Back	4 x 50	
Breast		3 x 30
Free		4 x 50

The same can be done for other stretchcord workouts. Breaststroke kicks can be added in the AM, while squats are scheduled for the PM. Wrist curls are a great way to finish off workouts and once a swimmer is in shape, they can be done to max (at the end of the workout).

The first few weeks it is advised that swimmers do rotate their strokes for a few reasons. Rotating strokes helps swimmers learn all the techniques associated with each stroke. It also shares the load around the body, as different muscles are used in different ways for different strokes. This can prevent injuries that could occur from overuse of one muscle or joint. After the first few weeks of successful training, if swimmers want to concentrate on one stroke, say butterfly, then they should feel free to do so.

Off-Season Training

During the off-season (meaning no in-pool swim training is taking place), swimmers can prepare for the challenges of the up-coming season by doing stretchcord training. After their final big meet, swimmers often take time off of *any* training just to rest their minds. When they start back with a stretchcord training program, they should start slowly and build their off-season routine week by week. High school swimmers may only swim during high school season or may also swim summer club. In either case, their off-season may be several *months* long. College swimmers often swim year round with very little time out of the water. However, even the most committed swimmers will usually take some time off immediately after the end of a season. Stretchcord training is a great way for each and every one of these athletes to get into shape prior to the next season's start. As little as 10 minutes a day can give a swimmer a huge head start before swim practices and meets begin.

In general, *off-season training* is designed to get swimmers from out-of-shape to in-shape condition and ready to do swim workouts. It may also be designed to strengthen weak areas swimmers displayed during the previous swim season.

Because off-season stretchcord training is meant to start slowly, light resistance stretchcords should be used initially. Swimmers should be able to perform 50-100 cycles of butterfly pull before complete fatigue sets in. This can mean a different stretchcord from that used later on or a closer stance to the tie-off point (or standing on a stool if cords hang from above).

The first week of off-season stretchcord training (except for first-time users) should begin with something like:

5 x 30 pulls

These pulls should be done with a butterfly pulling motion and, of course, should be preceded with a warm-up, like internal and external shoulder rotations. The set can be repeated 5 to 6 days a week right from the start as long as swimmers feel no joint pain (muscles may be a bit sore or tight which is normal). Leg exercises should also be included, and can be interspersed throughout the set. For example, 30 butterfly pulls, 30 squats—repeat five times. Remember, these are with lighter resistance cords than usual. If a swimmer feels muscle pain that they believe is beyond normal muscle soreness, stretchcord training should be halted and a day or more of rest should be taken before starting back with an even lighter resistance. If the swimmer still experiences undue muscle pain or if the swimmer feels pain from within the shoulder, elbow or wrist joints, the swimmer should stop the exercises and consult a physician. The swimmer's coach should be highly involved in this process.

If the first week goes well, swimmers should add 10 to 20 pulls to each set for the second week. Other strokes can be added in as well. If the swimmer is a breaststroker, then breaststroke is a perfect choice. The same would go for backstrokers and freestylers. The adding of 10 to 20 pulls can continue until the swimmers get to 100 pulls. Swimmers can also add a second set of a stroke or strokes, performed later in the day—one set in the morning and one in the evening.

An option for those who don't like to *count* is to have a timer nearby. Set the timer for a specific time, say 60 seconds, and do butterfly pulls for 60 seconds. Using this method, swimmers can concentrate on form or anything else while performing the exercises rather than counting. If one is training to break two minutes in a race, then doing two-minute sets of stretchcord training is a great way to add specificity to a workout.

Now, for many swimmers this type of training is ideal. They love routine and this is an easy, routine set. For other swimmers, all this repetition quickly becomes monotonous. They need variety. So, after the second week, here are some sets to change things up:

1 x 50 pulls or kicks/squats
1 x 40 pulls or kicks/squats 1 x 20 pulls on knees (or ½ meter
    back if bending over) or kick/squats with higher resistance
1 x until fatigue pulls on knees (or ½ meter back)
       or
6 x IM (15 cycles of each stroke)
       or
3 x IM (30 cycles of each stroke)

Even better, swimmers and coaches should apply the lessons in this book and develop their own sets. For many athletes, it can be easier to stay with a program when an outside individual (like the coach) keeps accountability.

Base/Technique Training

As mentioned earlier, stretchcord training should stay one step ahead of swim training, with the exception that race-specific stretchcord training which can be done at most any time (ask the coach). So, during the base/technique phase of the swim season, swimmers generally want to be doing endurance work with their stretchcords. Endurance work on stretchcords means long sets and lots of pulling. One way to get this work is to decide the total number of stroke pull cycles to be accomplished in a day, and then figure how to divide those cycles. For example, say 400 pull cycles:

Monday	AM	PM
Int/Ext Rotation	25 each	25 each
Fly	30	30
Back	30	30
Leg work	30	30
Breast	30	30
Free	30	30
Leg ad/abduction	30	30
IM	80	80
Catches	30	30

IM = 20 cycles of each stroke

Strokes can be weighted differently if desired. Swimmers can work on specific strokes. For example, if a swimmer wanted to work on breaststroke, then every other day, that swimmer could do all or a majority of the pulls breaststroke. In general, this is straight out training and not very exciting. However, in this period of endurance training, nearly anything can work. Swimmers can take sets from some of their favorite swim workouts and adapt them to the stretchcords. Here is one example.

10 x 100 free hard with an easy 50 between, all on 2:15.

Donna wanted to make this swimming set into a stretchcord endurance set. It takes Donna approximately 28 freestyle stroke cycles (again right and left arm equals one stroke cycle) to complete a 100 freestyle, 14 for a 50 free. Since the 100 freestyle in the set is supposed to be hard, and the 50 free easy, Donna would do 28 freestyle stroke cycles with a more difficult (thicker) stretchcord followed by 14 stroke cycles with lighter (thinner) stretchcords. This exercise could also be done by moving further away from the tie-off point to increase the resistance. She would then take a period of rest between each hard-easy combination and continue on the next interval just as she would in the pool. Any set that can be swum can be reproduced in such a manner.

Another way to adapt this set is for swimmers to *time* how long it takes them to complete the 28 stroke cycles. In each progressive set, they attempt to descend their time, just as they might do in the water. Yet another variation would be to pull for say one minute, increasing the number of stroke cycles each interval (remembering to keep perfect form). Both of these adaptations give swimmers something other than the stretchcord pulling to think about. Obviously, this set can be done in other strokes as well. And don't forget the warm-up and other stretchcord exercises.

So now the challenge is to take favorite sets and adapt them into stretchcord workouts. This will keep motivation present and boredom at bay. The coach could suggest some sets to adapt if the swimmer finds imagination or expertise are lacking.

Race Specific Training

Since stretchcord training is meant to increase swimming speed and/or stroke rate in the water, it makes sense to use stretchcords to train for specific races. To train for a 100-meter long course butterfly race, a swimmer would first need to know the number of strokes they currently take in that race. Have a coach or spectator watch and count, or better yet video and count, both 1st and 2nd 50's. For this example, say the swimmer takes 25 stroke cycles (right and left arm equals one stroke cycle of all strokes) on the first length and 28 stroke cycles on the second length. The stretchcord set for the 100 fly would be 4 x (25 stroke cycles, rest three seconds in streamline, then 28 stroke cycles).

Stroke rate training can also be added. *Stroke rate* is the amount of time it takes a swimmer to complete one stroke cycle of a given stroke. If it takes this swimmer 30 seconds from the first butterfly stroke to the wall on the first length, then this is a butterfly stroke tempo of 1.20 seconds/stroke. Perhaps the swimmer would like to reduce this (Olympic males are around 1.10 seconds/stroke). So, this swimmer would practice at a 1.10 second/stroke pace which completes the 25 strokes in 27.5 seconds.

This set can be made even more specific. Swimmers who like to take dolphin kicks off starts and turns (say 8 and 6 kicks respectively), can simulate dolphin kicks by moving their hips back and forth or raising up on their toes at the same frequency (times per second) that they do in the water. If the swimmer likes to use a breathing pattern, like every other stroke, then the swimmer's head can be raised every second stroke cycle. Using these techniques can prepare swimmers for their races both mentally and physically.

The previous paragraph was written with the assumption that our swimmer could already correctly swim a 100 butterfly. If a swimmer has trouble with a breathing pattern, then a breathing pattern should be practiced during stretchcord sets. Or, if a swimmer wants to take six dolphin kicks off the turn, but hasn't done it in a race yet, then concentration and practice with stretchcords (and no breathing during the simulated dolphin kicking!) could help the swimmer learn to do it during a race. This is a situation where both mental and physical practices are combined together to produce the goal result in a race.

IM stretchcord sets have already been discussed, but none have been specific for an IM *race*. For this example, take a swimmer's number of strokes during a 200-meter long-course IM. Let's say that was 26 strokes butterfly, 24 stroke cycles of backstroke, 23 pulls breaststroke and 21 stroke cycles of freestyle. So, a stretchcord 200 IM would include a continuous set of these pulls. Like the above butterfly set, the IM set can be done with specific start and turn routines. Streamline, no-breath dolphin kicks can be mimicked for butterfly, backstroke and freestyle. A breaststroke-like pullout can be included in breaststroke. If this is done in a set format (5 x 200 IM), make sure there is sufficient rest between each complete IM (perhaps two minutes).

Race specific stretchcord training is not only specific to the race an individual wants to swim but to that particular individual. There will be different stroke counts, different tempos, etc. When a swimmer doesn't know what the small details of his or her race are or should be, ask the coach for advice. Then practice that race on the stretchcords.

As mentioned earlier, race-specific training can occur in any swimming phase from off-season to taper. At the end of one season, swimmers usually have a burning desire to improve themselves for the next big meet (which could be 6 months to a year away). Working specifically on the race they would like to swim six months early can help them swim the race correctly during meets in the upcoming season which, in turn, will help them with the big race at the *end* of the next season.

Taper

Depending on how long one tapers, perhaps no additional out-of-pool training, including stretchcord training should be done during a taper. During the taper phase (as in all phases, but especially in tapers), swimmers should ask their coaches about additional training. The last week of taper, some coaches don't want swimmers doing any work outside of the water. So, if a taper only lasts for one week, then probably no stretchcord training will take place.

But most tapers last longer than one week, and stretchcord training can enhance race preparation for specific swims. The taper period is a good time to really attack those fast twitch muscle fibers. To do so, make the resistance on the stretchcord so that no more than 20 pulls can be completed. This can be done by moving further away from the attachment point, using stiffer cords, or perhaps even using two sets of cords together. The idea is to bring the muscles to fatigue several times without taking too long to do it. Swimmers would still complete a warm-up set with internal and external shoulder rotations. Here is an example of a set for an IMer.

Int/Ext Rotations (25 each side)
    Rest
Fly to max
    Rest two minutes
Backstroke to max
    Rest two minutes
Breaststroke to max
    Rest two minutes
Freestyle to max

This would be the entire stretchcord workout for the day. If a swimmer is preparing for just one stroke, they might do the following:

Int/Ext Rotations (25 each side)
    Rest
Butterfly to max
    Rest two minutes
Butterfly to max
    Rest two minutes
Butterfly to max

If preparing for two strokes, swimmers can alternate strokes, say breaststroke then freestyle, then the next day start off with freestyle followed by breaststroke. Or, one day can be all freestyle, then the next breaststroke.

This intense, to-failure training is painful, but it also doesn't last too long and it is very effective in developing power. Intensely working the fast twitch muscle fibers can create much more muscle strength that will help propel the swimmer down the pool faster than ever before.

It might be thought that this type of training is only good for sprinters since it is designed to work fast twitch muscle fibers, and it is certainly easy to understand how such training will help swimmers of shorter events. The truth is that distance swimmers also need to strengthen their fast twitch muscle fibers. Longer races often come down to a sprint for the finish. The swimmer with the best-conditioned fast twitch muscles is likely to win that race.

One last thing when looking at these types of maximum effort workouts—they can be performed during almost any time of the year as a change of pace. Max effort stretchcord work can be performed once a week, every three days, or for a week straight once a month. Swimmers should do some experimentation during non-critical times of the year to see what they like or what works well for them.

Fun Training

There are some fun ways to mix things up with stretchcord training. One is called Pulldown Poker. For this game, take a shuffled deck of cards and fan them out face down on a table. Turn a card over and whatever the number on the card is, that is the number of pulls that must be done. If the card is a jack, that's 11 pulls, queens are 12, kings are 13 and Aces are 20. This game is more fun when two or more are playing. Parents and siblings make good playing partners. Even if they're not swimmers, they can just pull down on the cords. Another way to play uses the suits of the cards to designate the strokes and the number for the pulls. Clubs are butterfly, Spades are backstroke, Diamonds are breaststroke and Hearts are freestyle.

A variation of this game uses dice. Toss two or three dice. Whatever the total, that is the number of pulls to be completed. If strokes are going to be added, agree to a stroke rotation prior to beginning (such as IM order).

Other games can be incorporated and turned into stretchcord games. Play a game of Yahtzee® and your opponent has to perform the score you earn and visa versa.

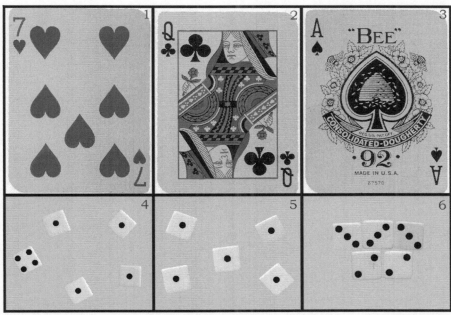

Stretchcord games. 1) 7 of Hearts is seven stroke cycles freestyle. 2) Queen of Spades is twelve stroke cycles butterfly. 3) Ace of Spades is twenty stroke cycles backstroke. 4) If this Yahtzee® roll is taken in ones it means 4 stroke cycles. If 4 of a kind, it is 8 stroke cycles. 5) A Yahtzee® (5 of a kind) earns a player 50 points and means 50 stroke cycles. 6) A full house earns a player 25 points and means 25 stroke cycles. If taken in 3s, it means 9 stroke cycles.

Imagination is the only limitation. Think what might be done with other favorite games. Fun training during the off-season and early season can add a nice change to the routine, though when preparing for a big meet, more specific training should take precedence.

NINE

TRIATHLON TRAINING

Adapting stretchcord training to triathlon is a simple matter. Triathlon training and stretchcords are near perfect for each other. This is because using stretchcords is like open water swimming—there is no end to the pool. Also, in triathlon swimming, the arms account for the vast majority of propulsion and stretchcord training is perfect for this. But stretchcords are also good for Triathletes for several other reasons. Triathlon is a very demanding sport that requires many hours of training a day. Time and distance to training sites become precious. Stretchcord exercises can be done quickly and virtually anywhere. Triathletes don't have to drive, change into a swimsuit, or go through the locker room process to train. They can simply go to their stretchcords, do a workout, and then hop right on their bike or step out the door for a run. Location is almost unlimited because stretchcords are portable.

Now, if you are a triathlete and have read up to this point, you might be thinking that this book really isn't written for you, it's written for swimmers. And many triathletes might turn to this section first, which is fine. But if you did that, go back to the other chapters and read them. Much of the information there will help you set up the best training plan for your triathlon swimming needs.

Certainly a very simple way to train for triathlon with stretchcords would be to get some fairly easy resistance stretchcords and build up to 900 stroke cycles. That, depending on the athlete, would be about equivalent to a 1500-meter open water swim for the Olympic distance triathlon. For the Ironman distance, at least double that stroke count. This kind of repetition pulling is not recommended on a daily basis, however, largely because it would be incredibly boring after only a few sessions. It's a good workout every once in a while, particularly if stretchcords are used to replace several swim workouts in a row.

So how does one train for triathlon using stretchcords? The question is not unlike the swimming question and should likewise be directed back to the athlete. As a triathlete, how do you currently train for the swim? That will provide your answer. Triathletes should use the knowledge learned in the previous chapters to tailor their own workouts. It is unlikely that triathletes get in the pool and swim 3600 meters or even 1500 meters straight every workout. If they did, they would be bored of swimming before too long, just as swimmers would, and they would not be optimizing their workout time.

So, use the examples given in the previous chapters to create your workouts. As an example, if a triathlete wanted to do a set of 5 x 200 free, it might be set up this way.

5 x (~60 stroke cycles)

There is no rule that says triathlon swimming must be all freestyle. It is efficient and fast, which is why it is most often the stroke employed in triathlon swimming. This does not mean, however, that it is the only pull pattern triathletes should practice. Swimming other strokes can help triathletes become better at freestyle if for no other reasons than that it helps increase their feel of the water and that all stretchcord training works the essential muscles of swimming propulsion. Additionally, working other stroke patterns during stretchcord training can greatly increase the variety of the workout. Butterfly stretchcord training is the most efficient and should probably be the staple of triathlon stretchcord workouts.

Triathletes who started as swimmers tend to swim all the strokes during practice either as force of habit or just to mix things up. Triathletes who do not have swimming backgrounds, however, may struggle with the other strokes, *especially* butterfly. Here is where stretchcord training can help pass along technique for the water. Once the butterfly stroke is perfected using *stretchcords*, it can be performed in the pool more effectively and with less difficulty. And it will improve your freestyle power as well. Butterfly in the pool (*or with stretchcords*) is a great way to build swimming strength that can help triathletes swim faster in any stroke.

In general, triathletes should use lighter resistance stretchcords and perform longer, endurance pull sets than their swimming counterparts. This alludes to the *specificity of training* concept. Triathletes can get faster by improving their endurance for the swim distance in this manner. However, once their endurance is adequate, they will need to increase their *power* to get faster. For this reason, triathletes should get two resistance levels of stretchcords, one for the long pull sets and another for power sets. Triathletes should be able to pull the low resistance cords over 200 times, the higher resistance ones only 25 to 50 times to full fatigue.

Having both sets will allow triathletes to alternate endurance workouts with power workouts. On the endurance days, triathletes might do sets of 4 x 100 stroke cycles freestyle while on the power days they might do the following:

    Int/Ext Rotations (25 each side)
        Rest
    40 butterfly pulls
        1 minute rest
    30 butterfly pulls
        45 seconds rest
    25 butterfly pulls
        30 seconds rest
    20 butterfly pulls
        30 seconds rest
    20 butterfly pulls
        and repeat until 20 pulls cannot be done

This type of workout will likely leave triathletes a bit sore the first couple of times, but if alternated with an endurance stretchcord workout, the soreness will subside after a few sessions.

The Freestyle Pull Pattern

When performing the freestyle pull pattern with stretchcords, athletes should use a catch-up stroke. A catch-up stroke is where both hands meet in the outstretched or streamline position before the next arm-pull begins. In other words, one arm makes its complete pull and recovery before the other begins and makes its full complete pull and recovery. Very few swimmers use a true catch-up stroke, hand touching hand before each arm pull. So a catch-up stroke used in the water most often refers to a *modified* catch-up stroke where one hand is in the streamline position while the other is in the "catch" position.

Is a swimming catch-up stroke or modified catch-up stroke good for every swimmer? No, it depends on the individual and the distance being swum. A general rule of thumb is that the longer the distance or the pool, the more effective a catch-up stroke will be. But there have been Olympic *50* Freestyle finalists who use catch-up strokes.

For distance swimming, a modified catch-up stroke is very useful because it can reduce drag. For this reason, some modified version of a catch-up stroke is a good bet for most triathletes. Stretchcord training is a great place to begin working on a modified catch-up stroke. Once it has been learned on the cords, it should be easier to implement in the water.

Here are some suggested main sets for triathlon stretchcord workouts. All workout-outs should begin with a warm-up set like Int/Ext Rotations (25 each side).

Endurance (low resistance)	Power (higher resistance)
100, 90, 80, 70, 60, 50, 50, 60, 70, 80, 90, 100 pulls either freestyle or butterfly. Rest between as needed	Max number of pulls x 5 with 1 minute rest between
6 x 100 pulls freestyle or butterfly. (Alternate lifting the head for 15 stroke cycles with keeping it down for 15 stroke cycles. This will help build the neck muscles needed for open water swimming.)	Max pulls minus 10, as many times as possible. 1-minute rest. Over time, as power increases, the max pulls should increase.

8 x (20 stroke cycles of freestyle followed by 3 seconds rest in the streamline position).	3 x 100 pulls with light resistance; each set is followed by a max pull set with high resistance. 2 minutes rest between
900 freestyle stroke cycles (approximately a 1500 meter open water swim)	Start with very heavy resistance and do max pulls, rest one minute, lighten the resistance slightly and do another max. Again wait one minute in between and repeat for a total of 5 sets.

TEN

WORLD CLASS STRETCHCORD ROUTINES

Perfection is something that most swimmers strive for. To this end, many swimmers attempt to emulate Olympic Champions and World Record Holders. Logically, if you copy the technique of someone who is successful, the expectation is that you also will be successful. In this chapter, stretchcord routines have been designed around analyses of the races of the top three Olympians in every event of the past Olympics. This should give readers tried and true examples to emulate. It can also be a good break from swimmers' usual sets.

This being written, it needs to be understood that swimmers will get more out of creating their *own* routines to match either the talents they currently possess or talents they wish to develop. Copying another's style does not take into account individual differences, and may fail to take advantage of untapped individual potentials. *Improvising* on another's routine to *personalize* it can lead swimmers to the top.

Each of the following routines adds the element of stroke rate. Again, *stroke rate* is the amount of time it takes a swimmer to complete one stroke cycle of a given stroke. For example, in breaststroke, if it takes a swimmer 1.60 seconds to go from streamline position through a pull and kick back to streamline position, then their stroke rate is 1 stroke per 1.6 seconds, which is often referred to as a stroke rate of 1.6. The best way to determine an individual's stroke rate is to count the stroke cycles over a certain distance (a length of the pool), time from first stroke to last stroke, and then take the average. Another method is to use a stopwatch and time a number of strokes in a length and take the average (some stopwatches have an average function that makes this very easy). Both of these methods start at the beginning of the first stroke (which might be as long as five seconds after the push-off).

Knowing stroke rate is important because stroke rate can be duplicated on stretchcords for a more specific and realistic effect and greater benefit. The stroke rates of the Olympic champions are listed. For swimmers to duplicate these stroke rates, they can have someone time them, purchase a stroke rate device (a small timer that beeps at preset intervals that can be worn inside a swim cap), or use a computer. Tempo trainers or "pacers" are highly recommended not only for stretchcord training, but also for swim training. A *metronome*, used for keeping music tempo could work for stretchcord tempo training if you already have one. The best solution for tempo stretchcord training is to make computer audio files to follow. These files can be downloaded to an MP3 player such as an iPod®. The audio files can be made to count strokes in perfect time, tell the swimmers when to hold their breath and streamline, when to rest, and when to switch strokes (IM). There are few limitations and all kinds of possibilities.

Stroke rates for stretchcord training may be different than stroke rates for actual swim training depending on the resistance in the stretchcords. Coaches often set dryland stroke rates between 5 and 10 percent faster than the swimming goal stroke rate. Depending on the stretchcord resistance used, readers should select their own training stroke rates for these types of sets. The Olympic stroke rates provided below can be good starting points.

Set pacers or metronomes to the stroke rates indicated or make more specific audio records including times to "hold breath-streamline-dolphin kick-change stroke", etc.

Women's 50m Freestyle
Stroke rate of 1.0

Take 22 stroke cycles (22 seconds). Use a stiff set of stretchcords and work the full length of the stroke. The Olympic Champion dove in and took 2.6 seconds before her first stroke.

Men's 50m Freestyle
Stroke rate of 1.0

Take 19 stroke cycles (19 seconds). Use a stiff set of stretchcords and work the full length of the stroke.

Interestingly, the men's and women's stroke rates (strokes per second) are the same for the 50 freestyle, but the men take fewer strokes per length. It is because they generate more force with each arm pull for a longer period of time (in part because their arms are longer).

"50 Free" Sets

6 x *50 free* on two minutes. Work on getting either the men's or women's complete and full stroke cycles in the time allowed. Also, limit breathing to once or twice (or even no breaths) during each 50. As one gets stronger, the set can be made more challenging by increasing the resistance.

3 x max number of pulls on three minutes—use two sets of stretchcords or make the resistance quite strong (so you are only capable of doing 20-30 cycles before exhaustion).

Women's 100m Freestyle
Stroke rate of 1.15

Take 20 stroke cycles (23 seconds), rest in the streamline position for about one second immediately followed by four dolphin kick-like motions (about three kicks/second) still in the streamline (do not breathe during this period). Immediately following the dolphin kicks, take 23 stroke cycles at the same rate. (Long course = two lengths.)

Men's 100m Freestyle
Stroke rate of 1.23

Take 17 stroke cycles (21 seconds), rest in the streamline position for about one second immediately followed by four dolphin kick-like motions (about three kicks/second) still in the streamline (do not breathe during this period). Immediately following the dolphin kicks, take 17 freestyle stroke cycles at the same rate.

"100 Free" Sets

5 x *100 free* on four minutes. Work on achieving complete and full individual arm strokes in the allotted time. Also, limit breathing to a pattern (like every four). Make the set more challenging by increasing the resistance.

4 x *100 free* as fast as you can take complete and full strokes (exaggerated stroke rate.) Two minutes rest between.

Women's 200m Freestyle
Stroke rate of 1.27

Take 22 stroke cycles (28 seconds), rest in the streamline position for about one second immediately followed by four dolphin kick-like motions (about three kicks/second) still in the streamline (do not breathe during this period). Continue with three more identical repetitions including the same streamline and dolphin kick-like motions between each 22 stroke cycles.

Men's 200m Freestyle
Stroke rate of 1.25

Take 20 stroke cycles (25 seconds), rest in the streamline position for about one second immediately followed by four dolphin kick-like motions (about three kicks/second) still in the streamline (do not breathe during this period). Continue with three more identical repetitions including the same streamline and dolphin kick-like motions between each 20 stroke cycles.

"200 Free" Sets

2 x *200 free* on 5 minutes (with higher than normal resistance)
5 x *200 free* on 4 minutes

Women's Distance Free
Stroke rate of 1.20

Take 25 stroke cycles (30 seconds), rest in the streamline position for about one second immediately followed by two dolphin kick-like motions still in the streamline (do not breathe during this period). Repeat this until the 'distance' desired has been completed. A 400 free would take eight repetitions, an 800 free 16 repetitions, and a 1500 free 30 repetitions of the 25 stroke cycles. Remember the "turn push-off" streamline and kicking.

Men's Distance Free
Stroke rate of 1.35

Take 20 stroke cycles (27 seconds), rest in the streamline position for about one second immediately followed by two dolphin kick-like motions still in the streamline (do not breathe during this period). Repeat this until the 'distance' desired has been completed. A 400 free would take eight repetitions, an 800 free 16 repetitions, and a 1500 free 30 repetitions of the 20 stroke cycles. Remember the "turn push-off" streamline and kicking.

Distance Free Sets

400 free
500 free
800 free
1500 free

2 x 400 free with 3:00 rest
2 x 500 free with 3:00 rest
2 x 800 free with 5:00 rest

Women's 100m Backstroke
Stroke rate of 1.40

Start with 10 dolphin kick-like motions (do not breathe during this period). The 10 kicks should be done in just under four seconds (about three kicks/second). Take 17 stroke cycles (24 seconds), rest in the streamline position for about one second, then in that streamline position take 12 dolphin kick-like motions (do not breathe during this period) followed by another 17 stroke cycles. Note: If you skip ahead to the men's 100 backstroke, you will notice that the men are required to take more strokes per length than the women. This is not a mistake. In fact, all of the top men (as of this writing) take more strokes than the top women.

Men's 100m Backstroke
Stroke rate of 1.0

Start with 12 dolphin kick-like motions (do not breathe during this period). The 12 kicks should be done in four seconds (about three kicks/second). Take 20 stroke cycles (20 seconds), rest in the streamline position for about one second, then in that streamline take 12 dolphin kick-like motions (do not breathe during this period) followed by another 20 stroke cycles.

"100 Back" Sets

5 x *100 backstrokes* on 4 minutes. Work on getting complete and full individual arm strokes in the time required. Make the set more challenging by increasing the resistance.

4 x men's or women's total stroke cycles (40 for men, 34 for women) as fast as you can while keeping proper form. Two minutes rest between. Keep track of your best *time* average in the set.

Women's 200m Backstroke
Stroke rate of 1.50

Start with 10 dolphin kick-like motions (do not breathe during this period). The 10 kicks should take just under four seconds (about three kicks/second). Take 20 stroke cycles (30 seconds), rest in the streamline position for about one second, then in that streamline position take eight dolphin kick-like motions (do not breathe during this period) followed by another 20 stroke cycles. Complete two more times with the same rest and dolphin kick-like motions between each set of 20 stroke cycles.

Men's 200m Backstroke
Stroke rate of 1.33

Start with 10 dolphin kick-like motions (do not breathe during this period). The 10 kicks should take just under four seconds (about three kicks/second). Take 18 stroke cycles (26 seconds), rest in the streamline position for about one second, then in that streamline position take eight dolphin kick-like motions (do not breathe during this period) followed by another 18 stroke cycles. Complete two more times with the same rest and dolphin kick-like motions between each set of 18 stroke cycles.

"200 Back" Sets

2 x *200 back* on 5 minutes (with higher than normal resistance)
5 x *200 back* on 4 minutes

Women's 100m Breaststroke
Stroke rate of 1.13

Start with a streamline and an underwater pull-like movement. This should take five seconds. Then take 23 breaststroke pulls (26 seconds), hold streamline for about three seconds and do an underwater pull, then take 27 strokes (30 seconds). Note: During each stroke, the streamline position should be held as long as possible while still maintaining the stroke rate. So do the pulling and recovery part quickly.

Men's 100m Breaststroke
Stroke rate of 1.21

Start with a streamline and an underwater pull-like movement (do not breathe during this period). This should take five seconds. Then take 19 breaststroke pulls (23 seconds), hold streamline for about three seconds and do an underwater pull (do not breathe during this period), then take 23 strokes (27 seconds). Note: During each stroke, the streamline position should be held as long as possible while still maintaining the stroke rate. So do the pulling and recovery part quickly.

"100 Breast" Sets

5 x *100 breaststrokes* on four minutes. Work on getting complete and full arm pulls to the belly button in the time required. Make the set more challenging by increasing the resistance.

4 x max number of pulls with double stretchcords, higher resistance stretchcords or increased resistance with current stretchcords. Two minutes rest between.

Women's 200m Breaststroke
Stroke rate of 1.50

Start with a streamline and an underwater pull-like movement (do not breathe during this period). This should take five seconds. Then take 20 strokes (30 seconds), hold streamline for three seconds and do an underwater pull (do not breathe during this period). Repeat three more times, 20 strokes with the simulated underwater pull between each set of 20. Note: During each stroke, the streamline position (the "glide") should be held as long as possible while still maintaining the stroke rate.

Men's 200m Breaststroke
Stroke rate of 1.55

Start with a streamline and an underwater pull-like movement (do not breathe during this period). This should take five seconds. Then take 18 strokes (28 seconds), hold streamline for three seconds and do an underwater pull (do not breathe during this period). Repeat three more times, 18 strokes with the simulated underwater pull between each set of 18. Note: During each stroke, the streamline position should be held as long as possible while still maintaining the stroke cycle.

"200 Breast" Sets

2 x *200 breast* on five minutes (with higher than normal resistance)
5 x *200 breast* on four minutes

Women's 100m Butterfly
Stroke rate of 1.10

Start with 12 dolphin kick-like motions in four seconds (three kicks/second) (do not breathe during this period). Then take 20 strokes (22 seconds), rest in the streamline position for about one second, then in that streamline position take nine dolphin kick-like motions in three seconds (do not breathe during this period) followed by 24 strokes (26 seconds). A breathing pattern (like every other stroke) can be used during this exercise.

Men's 100m Butterfly
Stroke rate of 1.11

Start with 12 dolphin kick-like motions in four seconds (three kicks/second) (do not breathe during this period). Then take 18 strokes (20 seconds), rest in the streamline position for about one second, then in that streamline position take nine dolphin kick-like motions in three seconds (do not breathe during this period) followed by 20 strokes (22 seconds). A breathing pattern (like every other stroke) can be used during this exercise.

"100 Fly" Sets

5 x *100 fly* on 4 minutes. Work on getting complete and full arm strokes well past the hips in the time required. Make the set more challenging by increasing the resistance.

4 x max number of pulls with double stretchcords, higher resistance stretchcords or increased resistance with current stretchcords. Two minutes rest between.

Women's 200m Butterfly
Stroke rate of 1.12

Start with nine dolphin kick-like motions in three seconds (three kicks/second) (do not breathe during this period). Take 25 butterfly strokes (28 seconds), rest in the streamline position for about one second, then repeat the sequence three more times (with the simulated dolphin kicks and no breathing during those kicks). A breathing pattern (like two up, one down) can be used during this exercise.

Men's 200m Butterfly
Stroke rate of 1.18

Start with nine dolphin kick-like motions in three seconds (three kicks/second) (do not breathe during this period). Take 22 butterfly strokes (26 seconds), rest in the streamline position for about one second, then repeat the sequence three more times (with the simulated dolphin kicks and no breathing during those kicks). A breathing pattern (like two up, one down) can be used during this exercise.

"200 Fly" Sets

2 x *200 fly* on five minutes (with higher than normal resistance)
5 x *200 fly* on four minutes

Women's 200m IM
Fly stroke rate of 1.27
Back stroke rate of 1.50
Breast stroke rate of 1.70
Free stroke rate of 1.38

Start with nine dolphin kick-like motions (three kicks/second—do not breathe during this period). Take 22 butterfly strokes (28 seconds—simulate a breathing pattern, like every other stroke), rest in the streamline position for about one second and do six dolphin kick-like motions in two seconds (no breathing). Then take 20 backstroke cycles (30 seconds), hold streamline for about three seconds and do an underwater breaststroke pull (no breathing). Then take 20 breaststroke pulls (34 seconds) and go back to the streamline position and do three fast dolphin kick-like motions (no breathing) before completing 21 stroke cycles of freestyle (29 seconds).

Men's 200m IM
Fly stroke rate of 1.22
Back stroke rate of 1.33
Breast stroke rate of 1.50
Free stroke rate of 1.33

Start with nine dolphin kick-like motions (three kicks/second—do not breathe during this period). Take 18 butterfly strokes (22 seconds—simulate a breathing pattern, like every other stroke), rest in the streamline position for about one second and do nine dolphin kick-like motions in three seconds (no breathing). Then take 18 backstroke cycles (24 seconds), hold streamline for about three seconds and do an underwater breaststroke pull (no breathing). Then take 20 breaststroke pulls (30 seconds) and go back to the streamline position and do three fast dolphin kick-like motions (no breathing) before completing 18 stroke cycles of freestyle (24 seconds).

IM note: All the stroke rates are listed for the IMs. The best way to accommodate the changing stroke rates of IMs is with a computer-based device as described at the beginning of the chapter.

"200 IM" Sets
2 x *200 IM* on five minutes (with higher than normal resistance)
5 x *200 IM* on four minutes

Women's 400 IM
Fly stroke rate of 1.18
Back stroke rate of 1.50
Breast stroke rate of 1.50
Free stroke rate of 1.30

Start with six dolphin kick-like motions (three kicks/second—do not breathe during this period). Take 22 butterfly strokes (26 seconds), rest in the streamline position for about one second, and repeat the sequence starting with the kicks. Then for the backstroke, rest in the streamline position for about one second before taking six dolphin kick-like motions (three kicks/second—no breathing) followed by 20 strokes (30 seconds) and repeat. For breaststroke, hold streamline for about three seconds and do an underwater pull (no breathing), then take 22 strokes (33 seconds) and repeat. Finally, go back to the streamline position and do three fast dolphin kick-like motions (no breathing) before completing 23 stroke cycles of freestyle (30 seconds) twice.

Men's 400 IM
Fly stroke rate of 1.22
Back stroke rate of 1.44
Breast stroke rate of 1.50
Free stroke rate of 1.44

Start with six dolphin kick-like motions (three kicks/second—do not breathe during this period). Then take 22 butterfly strokes (26 seconds), rest in the streamline position for about one second, and repeat the sequence starting with the kicks. Then for the backstroke, rest in the streamline position for about one second before taking six dolphin kick-like motions (three kicks/second—no breathing) followed by 18 stroke cycles (26 seconds), and repeat. For breaststroke, hold streamline for about three seconds and do an underwater pull (no breathing), then take 20 strokes (30 seconds) and repeat. Finally, go back to the streamline position and do three fast dolphin kick-like motions (no breathing) before completing 18 stroke cycles of freestyle (26 seconds) twice.

"400 IM" Sets

2 or 3 x *400 IM* on 7:00
1 x *400 IM* with higher resistance (one in the AM and one in the PM)

ELEVEN

STRETCHCORD WRAP-UP

Having adopted the saying, "Give a man a fish and feed him for a day or *teach* a man to fish and feed him for a lifetime," this book was designed to teach swimmers "how to fish". Swimming is an individual sport and every swimmer's training needs are different (from the 80-year old masters swimmer, to the 12-year old age-grouper, to the 44-year old triathlete). No single workout can be written that will help all swimmers achieve their maximum potential. There is no one thing that works for everyone. This book was designed to give each reader the knowledge to set up effective, self-tailored stretchcord workouts—in essence, teaching you, the reader, to "fish".

Having said that, this book does attempt to provide some extra help for specific workouts in its final section, "World Class Stretchcord Routines", with stroke counts and timing for each stroke and distance, calculated based on medal winning performances from the last Olympics. Use these workouts if you run out of ideas or modify them to fit your needs.

Stretchcords provide some of the best dryland exercises for swimming. Stretchcord training can replace time spent in the water for conditioning and stroke work because the movement patterns are so similar to actual swimming. This can be true for all four competitive strokes.

Stretchcord workouts are only limited by a swimmer's creativity. Swimmers can use different strengths of cords at different times or they can vary the distance from the tie-off point. Cords can be tied from above, in which case swimmers can pull from a standing position or on their knees, or from in front, where swimmers bend over. Two swimmers can do stretchcords at the same time with two sets of cords. Parents can do stretchcord workouts with their swimmers (this is highly encouraged). Thousands of different stretchcord workouts are possible. The results should be stronger, fitter muscles that should generate faster swimming.

Stretchcord workouts can also mirror specific swimming workouts. Sets of stretchcord pulls can be done on intervals. Strokes can be mixed in, including sets of IMs. Almost any swimming set that can be done in the water can be duplicated on land using stretchcords.

Here is one final caution about stretchcords. They will not last forever and should be inspected on a regular basis. A weekly inspection is prudent. When a set of stretchcords seems to be aging, drying out or turning a lighter color, it's time to replace it. In general, stretchcords should last a year or longer. The highest strength cords (thickest) place a lot of stress on their component parts and those components may fail after thousands of repetitions. Take it from the author—someone who has performed over 1,000,000 stretchcord pulls. It is best to replace your stretchcords before they snap. I've had my share snap before I started keeping better tabs on their condition.

So, be smart, be inventive, and pull on to faster swimming.

REFERENCES

Arata, A. (2003). *The Parents' Guide to Swimming.* 1stBooks, Bloomington, IN.

Riewald, S. & Cinea, K. (2003). Strength training for young athletes. *Olympic Coach.* **13** (1): 8-10.

Gonyea, W. J., Sale, D. G., Gonyea, F. B. & Mikeski, A. (1986). Exercise induced increase in muscle fiber number. *European Journal of Applied Physiology,* **55**, 137-141.

Wilmore, J. H. & Costill, D. L. (1994). *Physiology of Sport and Exercise.* Human Kinetics, Champaign, IL.

GLOSSARY OF TERMS

Aerobic – in the presence of oxygen

Aerobic Training – exercise that improves the oxygen-based energy producing systems and increases muscular and cardiovascular endurance

Anaerobic – without oxygen

Anaerobic Training – exercise that improves the non-oxygen-based energy producing systems and increases muscular power, muscular strength and muscular endurance

Concentric Muscle Contraction – the shortening of a muscle while work is being done

Dryland Swim Training – any training that takes place out of the water, the purpose of which is to make the swimmer faster, stronger and more resistant to injury

Eccentric Muscle Contraction – the lengthening of a muscle while work is being done

Endurance – the ability to continue work while resisting fatigue

Fast Twitch Muscles – large muscle fibers best at producing powerful movements through anaerobic means

Fatigue – the inability to continue exercise movement

Hyperplasia (muscular) – an increase in the number of muscle cells

Hypertrophy (muscular) – an increase in the size and/or weight of muscle cells

Interval Training – multiple exercise bouts with rest periods between

Isokinetic – where movement speed stays the same even when additional force is applied

Mitochondria – the organelles within cells where energy is produced aerobically

Muscular Endurance – the ability to repeat an exercise while resisting fatigue

Muscular Power – determined by how *quickly* one can move a workload

Muscular Strength – determined by the workload one can move

Overload – placing more stress on the body than the body is accustomed to

Overtraining – training beyond the physical and/or mental ability to recover

Periodization – the breaking up of a training season into phases, from getting-started (coming off of vacation) to the big end of season competition

Slow Twitch Muscles – muscle fibers with many mitochondria that use oxygen to produce energy and are resistant to fatigue

Specificity of Training – the idea that the physical response to training is directly related to the training activity

Stretchcords – bands that provide resistance when stretched

Stroke cycle – a full stroke where both arms have returned to the same position they started.

Stroke Rate – the amount of time it takes a swimmer to complete one stroke cycle of a given stroke.

Taper – a reduction in workload aimed at giving the body and mind a chance to recover from the rigors of training in order to perform at a peak level

ABOUT THE AUTHOR

Doctor Alan W. Arata holds a B.S. in Engineering, an M.S. in Exercise Science and a Ph.D. in Biomechanics. The son of a swimmer and swim coach, Dr. Arata started his swimming career at the "very old" age of 15, but at age 17 won a High School State Championship. After a Division I collegiate swimming career, he competed in and later coached Modern Pentathlon (swimming, running, fencing, shooting and equestrian). Dr. Arata has coached at the NCAA Division I level in two different sports, netting four NCAA trophies. He is the author of, *The Parents' Guide to Swimming* and several research articles. He is married to the former Kimberly Dunlop, a nine-time Modern Pentathlon National Champion. They have two children who are both age-group swimmers. Dr. Arata is a retired Professor of Biology and Physical Education and coaches USA and high school swimming.

NOTES

NOTES

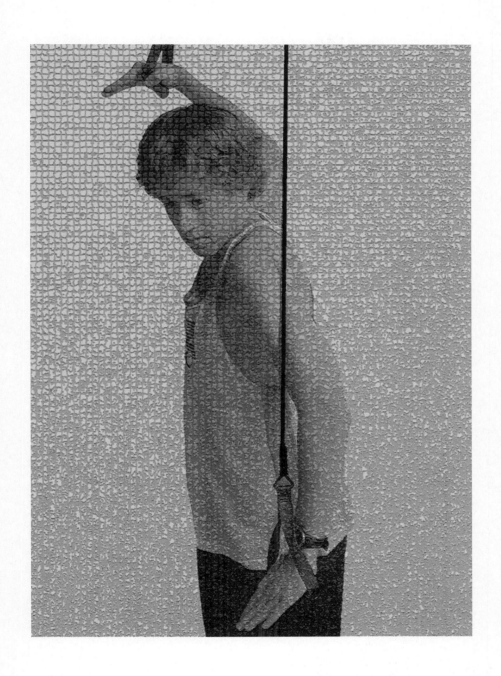

Printed in Great Britain
by Amazon.co.uk, Ltd.,
Marston Gate.